Our Greatest Treasures

All rights reserved. No part of this publication may be reproduced, stored in a retrieval system, or transmitted in any form or by any means—electronic; mechanical; photocopy; recording; or otherwise—except for brief quotations in printed reviews, without the prior permission of the publisher
Printed in The United States Of America

Copyright © 2009 Gerry and Dodi Pratt
All rights reserved.

ISBN 1-4392-3174-5
EAN 13 : 978-1439231746
To order additional copies, please contact us.
BookSurge
www.booksurge.com
1-866-308-6235
orders@booksurge.com

Our Greatest Treasures

Gerry and Dodi Pratt

PEPCO PUBLISHING
67A Dorr Drive
Rutland, Vermont 05701

2009

Contents

Introduction:	ix
1. RAISING CHILDREN IS AN UNSELFISH TASK	1
2. THE HOME FRONT (WHAT A CHILD LEARNS AT HOME	9
3. HEALTH CONCERNS	25
4. THE BEST BANG FOR YOUR BUCK	41
5. DISCIPLINE	61
6. TIME MANAGEMENT	77
7. STANDARDS AND CONVICTIONS	91
8. EDUCATION	109
9. ENTERTAINMENT AND HOW IT CAN AFFECT OUR CHILDREN	127
10. FRIENDS, SOCIALIZATION, AND DATING	147
11. SUBMISSION	165
12. POTPOURRI	179
13. SOME GENERAL THOUGHTS ABOUT RAISING CHILDREN IN CHRIST	195

Special Thanks

My wife, Dodi, who did the "lion's share" of the work in raising our children. To the Sunday morning Bible study class at Christ's Church of North Enid. And to Jessica Hays and Dodi Pratt, who helped proofread the manuscript. To Jessica, Tanager, Corinne, Andrew, and Danielle....our children. To all of our friends and relatives who had such a great input in helping our children to form some of their values and standards.

Introduction

The whole idea for this book came as a result of a request for a class in "child rearing". As I sat down to formulate this class, it became quite evident that there was far too much material for a class (unless we wanted a two or three year, in depth study of the subject). My next thought was of a book, but I felt so inadequate for such an undertaking. I know how many mistakes I have made over the years in raising my own children. It is only by the grace of God and His Spirit working in these children that they have turned out so successfully. I did have experience, however, and I did learn many things from the mistakes that I had made (albeit, sometimes way too late for my children's benefit). Therefore, this book is not a record of perfect parents doing everything perfectly. This book is a record of parents who tried to do right and the fruit of that endeavor. You may take advantage of the hard learned lessons, or you may experiment and learn your lessons first hand. I would hope that you would take the first course, for your sake.

Many of these lessons that I had to learn, my wife (Dodi), already knew. This book is also a tribute to her. Many of my mistakes were kept from being tragedies by her personal intervention. So many of these scenarios were real life problems that my loving wife and I encountered and the solution to the problem often came from Dodi.

To learn from other's mistakes amounts to great wisdom. If they have forewarned us and we choose to ignore these lessons, this would amount to a great deal of pride and folly. For the children's sake, I pray that wisdom would win the day.

For all you, who dearly love to read articles to find typos, I have purposely tried to make you happy and have left some in.

Gerry and Dodi Pratt

Chapter 1
Raising Children is an Unselfish Task

Raising children can be...NO...IS...one of the most selfless things that can be done by mankind. First of all, we deal with all of the problems and adjustments of a couple trying to make their marriage work. Then we mix into this selfless and demanding role, the raising of children.

Don't get me wrong...I think that raising children is the most rewarding thing that any couple could do. The love that you share with the "cutest" creatures in creation; the cuddles...the times of exploration for both the little one as well as the parents. The idea that you are doing the will of God can also be a rich reward of its own.

That being said, we do want to take a long drink from the cup of reality. You will sacrifice many times and in great ways. If your attitude or your frame of mind centers on only the negative, you can make yourself the most miserable person on Earth. That seldom happens, however, because most people kind of know all that I have said thus far. We prepare ourselves (as much as is possible) for this little child who will become the focus of all of our attention, for some time.

Use the Bible as your best guide Book. There are books written by mankind that can also be of help. It is to that end that I try to relate to you what we've learned.

Certainly, we all need to weigh everything and make some final choices in what we are willing to accept as a part of living. The unselfish ones will accept a certain amount of responsibility towards each other; the human race; and especially towards God's will. God wanted mankind to "Go forth and replenish the earth..." To do this, we must understand that there may be some sacrifices which we must make.

When the two of you became one, in marriage, the selfish parts of you really did have to give in to someone else. The reasons our marriages are so unstable is that this commitment was not really made in the hearts of all. If we claim to be Christian, we need to see what this claim does to us. It puts us in the place of a sacrificer.

We sacrifice for the sake of God and our marriage partner. We also should have the heart of a sacrificer in regards to the raising of children, as well. We are no longer single. The wonderful feeling of sexual gratification in the marital relationship also carries with it some unselfish responsibility towards God to do His will and replenish the Earth for God.

Children come from a natural process that is started in and sustained through marriage. There have been other man made systems that can also cause a child to be born. The other systems may or may not bless the unselfish husband and wife team that biologically cannot have children. Praise the Lord that this can now be done. Again, however, to go to all of that effort doesn't indicate self- centeredness.

When we have children, we are affected socially. Some of the entertainment that singles and young couples may be able to participate in is now limited by the fact that you have become a family of three. One needs to consider the lateness of the hour for the sake of the child or children.

If we are really doing the best for our families, we need to consider the atmosphere that some of our previous activities lingered in. There is the real problem of "second hand" smoke getting into the very small and fragile lungs of the children. Even if you were willing to take the risks of "second hand" smoke on you and your mate before...we now have other responsibilities. I think that it is very selfish and a real form of child abuse to subject the lungs of your little children to it. You child(ren) should not have to be subjected to your poor (if not horrible) choices.

We could go on further in this regard to the unselfishness of having and raising children, but I want us to see some of the other things that we will either completely sacrifice. We will (should?) make some huge changes in how we have always operated.

We will also need to not fill up our social schedule so full, that we don't (can't?) spend the needed time with our children. To do anything, as husband and wife, we will have to sacrifice the money needed for baby sitting.

A little side note on baby sitters: These people have total charge of and care of your children when you are gone. What do you really know about this person? If you are doing your job, as a parent, you will want to know what kind of individual this person REALLY is. This takes work...lots of effort and a great deal of tact so that you do not insult the baby sitter's family.

How much are you willing to pay this person whom you have entrusted with your most precious treasures? You do know the old saying: "You get what you pay for", don't you? One of the reasons you're stuck with uncaring baby sitters, is because you don't show that you are really all that caring yourself.

Money is another sacrifice that comes with having children. I will deal with the whole money thing in a later chapter, but we will touch on it as it is one of the many sacrifices that you will be making...if you do it right. It does take a little more expense for each new child that you add to your family. I see so many people not wanting to have children right away, because they are afraid to not do financially right by their children. Just go ahead and do it! If you wait too long, you may pass up a window of opportunity that shall never come again. Your health may change before you can have children. What insures that waiting will build up the bankroll. Many times it does, but many times the goal is not met and the children do or don't eventually finally come, It is quite possible, if you wait too long, that you won't live to see them graduate from High School. This can produce tragic feelings of

Animals may "learn" something from trial and error, but the major part of their life is programmed by instinct, **NOT** learning.

People, on the other hand, are completely different. If you leave a baby on the floor, unattended, he will stuff **A N Y T H I N G** into his mouth!! Little boys and girls do not instinctively know how to ride bicycles. We teach our children what is good and what is bad. We do this because, sometimes bad things look good and good things may look (taste?) bad. We have to teach our children values because without teaching, the child will either have no values, or they will form the values from those who take the time to teach them; or will form values from life's experiences.

As Christians, we want our children to form Biblical values and standards. We want our children to grow up with values that are totally compatible with the Word of God. For the most part these values will not be coming from people who do not make the Bible a very important part of their lives. This seems quite obvious, but I am amazed, sometimes, at the number of Christians who feel that everyone else should teach their children (without regard to the values of the children's teachers). These same parents blame the church; the preachers; the other Christians; or the youth group when things don't go right!

Understandably there are times and circumstances when you are going to have to entrust your children to others. There are two points that are begging to be made here. First, make sure that YOU set the foundation for your children's values…BEFORE SOMEONE ELSE GETS THEM. If you are lazy and unconcerned and expect this child to somehow go on "auto pilot", someone will set those standards, and you may not like what you get. Point two: and it is somewhat related. Don't throw your children to the wolves. Know what your child is being taught outside the home, **AND BE DILIGENT TO CORRECT ANY WRONG TEACHINGS THAT YOUR CHILD IS RECEIVING OR HAS RECEIVED.**

Parents, stop being so trusting of strangers. Just because you may have had a good and wholesome learning experience outside of the home, when you were growing up, don't assume that your child is also receiving that kind of attention I don't know how to tell you this, but it is a whole different world out there from the one you grew up in.

Parents need to know exactly who their children's teachers are and what they believe and stand for. These teachers may have very good secular and scholastic credentials, but what about their moral values and behavior. Let me tell you, up front, that you will receive a good deal of resistance in trying to find these things out. Try to find out just what these teachers stand for (and against). To the best of your knowledge and understanding, whom are you letting form a great deal of this child's character? If you know about something negative, you and your mate should determine how bad an influence this will have on your child and if you are both willing to leave that child in that setting. You must understand that even in the best of situations, these people to some degree will put some of their values into their teaching. Just what is acceptable to you?

At this point we want to deal with another most important area of your child's understanding, a "good work ethic". Parents can set their children up for success or failure in life.

The best way to teach a good work ethic is by setting the example. Dad goes to work every day. He does not call in to the boss and lie. When dad is healthy, he does not try to portray that he is sick so that he can play a round of golf; take a trip; or just lie around the house in an irresponsible way. Children are watching. You may not realize just how much these little eyes and ears take in. You are saying to your child, "this is what daddy does when he grows up, this is the way to handle your work situation when you also grow up".

Mommy doesn't stay in bed until nine o'clock in the morning. Mommy has many things to do, such as: fixing breakfast; doing the laundry; transporting children; cleaning the house; preparing supper, and the list goes on and on. The children see that a mother has a work ethic, as well (even though they may not know what to call it).

Your little girl will know that mommy does a lot of things around the house. She knows this, not because mommy taught a class in "homemaking 101".

Chapter 2
The Home Front
(What a Child Learns at Home)

What the child learns at home will be the gauge of his/her standards for the rest of life. The home is more than a place to play or a shelter from the rain. The home is a learning experience, as well. All too often we associate learning with formal classroom settings. This is true, but it is not the only form of learning. Any one form of learning is not especially superior to any other. We need to subject the child to a well rounded education.

Learning comes in many forms that are far removed from the classroom experience. Ideal child rearing would have most, if not all, of a child's learning under parental guidance. If the child learns at school, the parents should show enough interest to go over what that child is learning. There may need to be some clarification of what the child has been given to understand. The way things are going today, the educational institutions are not encouraging parental participation. Participate anyway!!

When the little girl stands on a chair and watches her mother bake a cake, she is learning. When a little boy hands daddy a wrench as daddy fixes the car, he is also learning. When the children are allowed to observe bugs; ants; and other creatures from the catalog of God's great creation, they are learning.

Children **WILL LEARN**. It is very important that they learn what is right and good. This is where you, as parents, come into the picture. God has designed the family in a way that each child will grow up with two teachers. This is a very good thing. Contrary to what others may want you to believe, we are not animals. Animals are born with "instinct". A baby bird knows how to fly. It may seem that mamma bird is "teaching" her little ones, but she is simply prodding them to do what she instinctively knows to be true.

"My darling feathered children know how to fly. Let me just boot them out of the nest so that they can discover this fact". Frogs do not go to "jumping" school or to "bug eating" school...they just know.

A carnivore doesn't waste his time on berries and a vegetarian doesn't even sniff at meat. They all just know. There are even foods that may harm or even kill some of these animals. How do they know not to eat these foods? Instinct.

Why do people imagine that animals are like people? Some even have worked with different animals so as to understand that the animal is "speaking". These same people would apply human feelings and other human attributes to animals...WHY?

Ever since the theory of evolution has found a footing in the educational system, people (so called...scientists) have attempted to make humans and animals all the same. They try to do this by "smarting" the animals and dumbing down the humans. Animals did not have God make them in His image and after His likeness, as he did with mankind. We are not the same physically and certainly not the same spiritually. Jesus Christ **DID NOT DIE ON THE CROSS FOR ANIMALS!**

parents keep an eye on this movement. This theory is being pushed and textbook publishers are co-operating in this agenda.

Another thing that is happening in the public school system, is that there is an organized attempt to cut the parent out of the picture. Quite a few times, now, schools have attempted to teach "sex education" along with morals and standards that fly in the face of Christian beliefs and practices. If you send you children to public school follow up on what they are learning.

At the risk of repeating what I will say in a future chapter in this book...let me make a firm and clear statement concerning schools: There are, as this book goes to press, three basic forms of education.

1. Public School education from elementary to secondary and even into college.

2. Christian education comes in many different forms using many different curriculums. Most call for a very well charted course. This form of education can and does cover the same span of grades. 3. Home schooling. This form of schooling takes place in our private homes. It greatly depends upon the parent as to how good this education can be. It also can cover the same spectrum of grades because the home schools can use curriculum from the Christian school system. Now there is even material printed specifically for the home school.

All can do a great job...if...the parents will be involved. Parents need to go over what has taken place during the school day in either the Christian school or public school situation. Parents can not let up their guard just because they have great faith in a form of education. Bad things can and do happen even in protected settings. The reason that I did not include the Home School situation is because the parent inadvertently **MUST BE COMPLETELY INVOLVED!!** As some old sage once said: "You can expect what you inspect"...and this is very true.

Another lesson to be taught at home is how to handle our emotions. If it is not taught at home it will be displayed in public. Far too many parents let their children down in this area. These same children are expected to live and function in the real world while not being able to get a grip on their anger; their jealousy; their covetousness. One is not properly preparing their children for life when they refuse to deal with the child's emotions and how they display those emotions. You are not properly preparing your children for life if you will not deal with your own emotions and be able to set the example of how to handle the various frustrations of life.

Certainly the best way to teach your children is to practice good emotion control, yourself. It is quite possible that your parents left you unprepared for life. Your father or mother may never have dealt with your fits of anger and impatience. Don't you think that it is time to break this damaging cycle? We need to make every effort to control our emotions and set the proper example for our children. Why would anyone want to damage their children because of some kind of fear or some kind of pride that will lock these little ones in an extremely destructive means of dealing with life?

Self control is what the Scriptures refer to as this worthy practice. As with other things, if you can get control of your anger, you will get control of some of the other problem areas of your life.

Moms and dads need to bite their tongues until they bleed...the children are there, watching. If you are bitter and resentful towards others...the children are watching. If you can see something that you want and verbalize out loud your intentions, "I don't really need that and I certainly can do without it". Know this, the children are watching, and seeing, and hearing.

If you have just recently started the battle for self control, you might even humble yourself and let the children know how hard the struggle is. They can remember all of this when they normally don't get a good handle on this thing of "self control". This is something that they would do best to learn when they are young...it doesn't get easier as they get older. Ask for your children's prayers and let them know that you are praying for them, as well.

Sometimes we can relate to our children a personal story of victory over self. "I think that I can understand how you may feel, a little bit. Remember how that man called mommy fat? I felt terrible for a while. As I had time to think about it, I had to admit that perhaps I was overweight and I did need to start watching my diet.

So you see, I actually was being helped by what that man said, even though I hurt for a while I was angry for a short time, but I could use what he said for something good. I also know that God loves me even if I don't succeed and get all the weight off that I need to".

By relating this story to your child, you give him/her something to "hang their hat on". You have set a very important standard for your children. Your child knows that it is not constructive to get and remain angry. Your child realizes that he/she may be able to turn this thing that made him angry, around. This whole incident can become a good guide for the future incidents of this kind (and there will be some). Your child is learning not to become bitter and vengeful. "Bitterness and vengeance will I destroy". Your children watch and they do listen, but the most important part is, **THEY WILL IMITATE YOU.**

This leads me to my next point. Just how **DO** we treat others? We want to teach our children the Christian perspective. The old and well worn question, "What would Jesus do"?, needs to be considered in each incident. It needs to be taught and it needs to be set as an everlasting habit. Children often pick up bad habits...what about a good one, for a change?

I don't know how to tell you this. Your children are just naturally selfish. Yes, your darling little child thinks only of himself/herself. You can see it when children play together. You can see it, that is, if you haven't blinded yourself to the truth.

Children need to be taught to share things with each other. Parents can make an excellent object lesson for their children by bringing the children along when mom and dad share. Just a word of caution here, make sure that the children know to not tell others that you have helped someone out. The more sharing you do, as parents, the more sharing your children will do.

It may be a fight, but **MAKE YOUR CHILD SHARE TOYS!** This may be their introduction to the concept of sharing with others. Your child will not naturally like this idea. You may find it necessary to punish the rebellion that usually occurs when you are trying to teach this concept. Be sure that you also reward the child when he/she shares. If you can teach this important lesson in the sandbox, you may have an easier go of it later on in more important situations.

Helping others in all areas of service needs to be taught to them by word and by your example. Let us look for ways to help out the other guy, and even involve your children in looking for ways to help specific individuals or families.

You and your children can sing at nursing homes, send cards to other people, perhaps you can babysit for a neighbor while she takes care of some important errand (such as a visit to the doctor's). Make it a fun time. You will feel richly rewarded by doing these things and you will teach your children a valuable lesson. God will certainly work through you and your children to bless others. If any thanks are returned, make sure to openly ask them to give God the glory.

Being considerate is a learned attribute. Some children are more inclined to be considerate than others, but they all need to learn these lessons. Consideration is when we forget about "self" and think of others, instead. Perhaps you can show it in different ways, but this is one that you need to instruct with words and by setting the example.

Turn the tables. Ask the child how they feel when good things are done for them or when other people are polite to them. Explain that other people have the same kind of feelings that we have. Try to bridge the gap and make the connection between our feelings and their response to others and their feelings. It is equally important to note their response to us when we are showing consideration to them.

If you, as the parent, can get the children to use their imaginations enough to imagine what the other person thinks and feels, you have won the "consideration battle". When they suggest something that may hurt someone else's feelings, you could say, "I don't think that I want to do that because I believe that they will feel badly". Hopefully they will make these same kind of connections without too much prodding.

The biggest thing in how we treat others is lumped up in how **YOU** treat others. Your example needs to set the standard. If you never had a good example set for you, work hard at breaking new ground. You can tell your children what is right, but you will completely destroy your words or you will validate your words...**BY WHAT YOU DO!**

Financial responsibility is also taught at home. Many believe in allowances (I don't. I don't believe that an allowance properly reflects real life. Nobody just hands a person money each week for nothing). I do believe in paying a child for some "special chores", however. We need to teach the proper use of this money. God needs to be thought of. The support of His work here on this Earth needs to be taught to our children. Some adults don't have a proper grip on this, themselves! If you believe in returning a tithe to God then teach this concept to your children. Later on, when they can reason and understand well, you may have to help the children to form a personal conviction on the subject of giving. Until then they need to just learn to do it. If you don't believe in a tithe, teach them how they **DO** support the work of God on this Earth.

If you have gotten across to them the concept of sharing, they may want to give some of their money to some other person or cause. Encourage this; it is a very good and commendable desire. Perhaps you can "adopt a child" in a foreign land and send this child some kind of support each month. Of course, you are going to put in the most money, but perhaps your children want to put in their dimes and pennies.

Honesty is so necessary. It is initially learned at home. How well it is learned at home will be a determiner of whether it sticks, at all. When some have gone into business, later on in life, it seems that their honesty was applied to a Teflon heart. Honesty is not just something you learn. **NO**, honesty needs to become a way of life.

A child needs to be taught honesty in all things and at all times and at all costs. Honesty cannot be "situational". One is not honest most of the time, but in some certain situations it is all right to lie. A child must be taught to tell the truth, even when it may get him/her in trouble.

Your child will be no more or less honest than you are. If you will lie to get out of tight situations, so will your child. Parents need to be honest to a fault (if there were ever a fault in it). Children pick up on this one **VERY QUICKLY. IF YOU LIE AND SEEM TO GET AWAY WITH IT...NO MATTER WHAT YOU HAVE SAID ABOUT TELLING THE**

TRUTH...you child will lie and expect to get away with it, also.

If your child lies, he/she **MUST BE PUNISHED!** Set the punishment in advance. Never deviate from this punishment for any reason. Beware though, if you are lying and getting away with it but punishing your child for the same behavior, you are going to raise a rebellious teenager and adult. Children are idealistic. They see things for what they are and for what they ought to be and they become very bitter and angry when the two do not match up. I believe that it is this very idealism that causes so many young people to leave the Church. The adults may talk a good talk, but the children view them as hypocrites when they teach one thing but do another. These children are not wrong!

Ephesians, chapter four and verse twenty nine tells us how our speech should be when we are addressing others. Our mouth will get us into more trouble than any other part of our body.

God's word says that you cannot praise and worship God with your tongue and at the same time curse men who are made in the image and likeness of Him. A fountain doesn't put out polluted water and fresh water from the same spigot. As hard as it is to do, we need to get control of our tongues and teach our children to get control of theirs, as well.

Our speech, and theirs, needs to be edifying. Do you talk just to hear yourself talk? If you have a child that does this, you are going to be a ripe candidate for the mental ward. The problem is that they may just be imitating you. Take a good look at yourself. Ask others if they think that you talk too much about inanities. Only if you can get control of your tongue, can you help your child get control of his.

Speech should be kind. Some of the previous things that we addressed come into play here. Consideration would teach kind speech. When children are not taught to be considerate, it shows up...DEFINITELY...in their speech. Love would constrain us to treat others with a view to their feelings. Love and consideration produce kindness: in speech and in actions.

Teach your child to speak things that make sense and ask questions that he/she really wants to know how. Watch out on this one, however, children do go through a period of time when they speak gibberish. As they get older, however, they need to leave the gibberish behind. If you don't do this, you will have a nine year old speaking gibberish. There comes a time in every child's life when he/she should be able to add to the conversation and not detract from it.

A lesson needs to be taught to parents, as well as children, about grace. Grace is where you "cut people some slack". You and I are capable of saying just about anything. Perhaps the person that you are speaking to deserves a good piece of your mind. Grace says that you don't give them that piece, but instead you give the peace. This is a hard concept to teach. Many parents do not subscribe to it, themselves, but it is important for your child to grow up and be a person that others want to have around. You have all seen and heard the overbearing, over critical and totally obnoxious judge of all humanity. Don't be one. Don't teach your child to be one by your over critical attitude.

This final teaching lesson relates to the previous one. Parents need to teach a lesson on forgiveness. You can do it in a multitude of ways. First, and foremost, you must set the example. What is forgiving? Forgiving is letting a wrong go. It is forgetting that it ever happened. It is treating that person who is the object of that forgiveness, with love.

If you don't learn how to forgive, you will become bitter, hateful, vengeful, and totally consumed. Those who cannot properly forgive are (at least for a time and in a specific way) deranged. Whatever this person cannot forgive grows. It gets so large that it consumes their life and dominates their mind. This person who isn't being forgiven, many times, may not even know what is going on in the mind of the non-forgiver.

These are hard lessons to learn for a little girl or a little boy. It is hard to forgive the little boy that pushed you down and ripped your dress. It is very hard for a little boy to forgive the other little boy who gave him a "fat" lip. At times like these, parents may even be caught up, emotionally, in the situation. Parents have been known to go to the father of the one that wronged their "precious child", and bloody their lip!

As hard as it might be on everyone, children need to learn to forgive. They need to learn it from you. They need to see it in action at home. They need to see it in action as you deal with your co-workers. They need to see it in action as you deal with **THEM**.

You are teaching them with your words; you must. You have to describe what forgiveness is. You must tell them how this is applied and relate to them some real life examples. Sealing your points, however, only comes in the demonstration of your love and forgiveness. You must be ready to ask for forgiveness from your children. Surely we have all made some mistakes in raising our children. Make sure that pride does not preclude you from teaching this important lesson. Your children are watching. Your children are learning. You can be absolutely sure of this.

What your children learn, at home, is wholly determined by you. They can learn things that you really don't want them to learn. They can learn good things: things that will hold them in good stead for the rest of their lives. They can learn about God and what He would have them do. I'm sure that you want your children to apply the motto, "What would Jesus do?" to their whole lives. This will go far to make sure that they are an asset to the community, and a pillar of the Church. What they become is most probably going to be a result of what you have taught them.

Chapter 3
Health Concerns

We are all concerned with our children's health. It is normal and right to be concerned, we need not to be ignorant in this critical area. Most of us are not nurses or doctors, but we still can educate ourselves on what is right and what might be dangerously wrong.

You can pick up several different books that deal with symptoms and treatment for minor health problems. There are, also, many helpful guides that cover nutrition and work on the preventative areas of health care. I would suggest that you pick one up that you can feel very comfortable with and use it extensively. It is very important to say this, however...if you have **ANY DOUBT**, see a doctor. These books are just there to give you general ideas. They are not the same as doctors and nurses. We need to keep this fact in mind when using them.

If there is not a whole lot of money available, and/or if there is not an affordable health policy in place, it just may be a temptation to try to doctor the problem, yourself. I do not recommend this course of action.

Even when this may be what you perceive as your only option, you might want to think some things through: 1. You may cause severe damage to your child. 2. You may make it necessary for your child to go to the hospital when, if he/she had gone to the doctor at the onset of the problem, he/she might have quickly recovered. 3. You may possibly leave yourself open to prosecution by the state for not giving your child the proper medical attention that the problem deserves. Benjamin Franklin had a saying for this that can be applied: "Penny wise and pound foolish". In the long run, what are you saving, and is the danger to which you are subjecting your child really worth it?

If you really cannot bring the child to a doctor because of finances, you may want to try some alternatives. Many cities and towns have a free clinic. Check into this for your family. You will have to snoop around to find this clinic. Ask others who do not have any insurance what they have found that works for them. Also, some states will give you free government insurance for either a small fee or no fee at all. You need to shop until you drop for this absolutely necessary guard for you and your family. Ask friends and relatives for suggestions. Don't give up on any possibilities for help along these lines.

Do not overreact. You can educate yourself on what should be considered serious and what isn't. We see the pendulum swing to the extremes in both directions. In the first scenario we find the parent with the book in one hand trying to perform open heart surgery on his child. On the other hand we have the parent all upset because her child has a nose bleed. I know that this is gross exaggeration, but, there are some scenarios that would come close. The "panic mode" can do a lot of damage and little to no good. If nothing else it passes along an attitude of fear to the child. This is the fuel from which phobias develop. Also, this undue and inappropriate fear can grow up with the child and a chain of phobias is started.

The second problem comes in when good and thoughtful treatments are passed up while a person is left "spinning their wheels". In some instances this vain and useless action can actually be dangerous. Education is the key to the proper reaction. Even though you may not be a doctor or a nurse, educate yourself as much as possible in all of the potentially dangerous scenarios. If your child has a history of one particular problem, pour yourself in to a better understanding of the treatment.

It is good for us to kind of know what we will do before we are called upon to do it. Also learn how to remain calm when you are going to try to help you child. The more you are properly educated, the more you will know when to go to the doctor and when you can handle it yourself. This being said, **WHEN IN DOUBT GO TO THE DOCTOR!**

Let us deal with some preventative options. **NUTRITION.** Some have gone way overboard in this thing of proper nutrition. I say this: better to go overboard than to damage and destroy your child's health by allowing them to eat non-foods (commonly known as "junk food"). Read the back of the box. It can be just that simple...read the label. If you can't pronounce it, or if you don't really know what it is, why would you want to feed it to your precious children? These chemicals are good for the manufacturer because it helps to keep things from rotting. **THEY ARE ONLY GOOD FOR THE MANUFACTURER!!** The best thing for you and your children is food that is as fresh and unprocessed as is possible.

Fresh fruits and vegetables are healthy. Make sure to wash all fruits and vegetables. There are multiple reasons for this: 1. Disease and various forms of filth can be on the surface of the produce. These fruits and vegetables handled by a multitude of people: farm workers, grocers, fellow shoppers, etc., etc.. 2. There can be residual pesticides on the skins of these fruits and vegetables. 3. Fruits and vegetables are not commonly exposed to steam baths or other cleaning processes that might remove unwanted "guests".

Uncooked is better than cooked (In some cases), but it really doesn't matter in the long run. The important thing is that your children are eating real food as opposed to something with a cheese taste and a consistency of Styrofoam. If it has been processed to the degree that you wouldn't know what it came from (if it wasn't printed on the label), probably it isn't real food.

The same goes for drinks. Our society has a love affair with sugar. Your body does need sugar, tis true. The whole truth is this: most everything that you eat turns to sugar. You do not really need to put refined sugar into your body. The less it is used the better for all. Try to steer your children away from food and drink that are loaded with refined sugars. Here is another one: fructose sweetener. It is not supposed to be good for you, but you are finding it in almost everything. Refined sugars do something that can be considered bad for your body.

Refined sugars or a lot of any kind of sugar will hype your children. After they are hyped up at breakfast time with all of the sugar, they are marched off to public school where they are given label such as **ADHD** and others. They are just super hyped kids that are not dealt with properly because we have taken discipline out of the schools!

Sugar....ANY KIND OF SUGAR...runs the blood sugar level way up and then drops **WAY DOWN**. This can translate to hypoglycemia or to hyperglycemia. Both of these can actually become fatal. When hyperglycemia (a by product of sugar diabetes) hits, it comes with some unwanted side effects. You, as a parent need to look up **Hypo- Glycemia** and **Hyperglycemia**. All of this translates to a child that is out of control and wild. With this comes the later problem that this child becomes so tired that he/she can't do anything. You are allowing your child's body to come under extreme stress. Especially is this true for their organs. See your doctor!

Fried foods are not good for you or you children. After saying that, I have to say that I love fried foods. Most Americans like fried foods, but the fried foods are not returning the favor. The bad part of all this is that there are so many other delicious ways to prepare food. We don't need fried.

Almost anything in the meat/fish category that can be fried, can be broiled; grilled; or baked just as well. Unless you have really developed a taste for fat and grease, your meats will taste so much better when broiled or baked. This you should know, your tastes **CAN** adapt.

The fried food problem comes from getting our foods already prepared for us. Fast food restaurants have a place in our life (rarely). If you are traveling, there is nothing so friendly as a well recognized fast food restaurant. You know just what to expect and you know the prices. At home, however, one would be foolish to stop at a fast food restaurant. They charge way more for their food that it would cost if you had prepared the same food at home. Fast food is also loaded with vitamin F (for **FAT**). Fast food restaurants are just plain unhealthy. The biggest problem with all of this is: 1. They taste good. 2. The children pester you to take them there (maybe not only for the food?). 3. It saves you from preparing things when you are tired, hot, out of sorts, etc., etc...Do not let these reasons win over your good sense.

The medical profession has slowly caught up to the importance of vitamins and minerals needed in our diet.

More than likely you will not be getting all of the vitamins and minerals that your body needs, simply by eating good foods. If this be the case, you must know that your children also will be short changed in this department...no matter how well they are fed. It is also important to note that not all health professionals and doctors agree with what constitutes a daily quota of vitamins and minerals that are needed.

I will tell you that I am not a great believer in: "If a little is good then a whole lot is a whole lot better". I believe that vitamins and minerals can become a fad phase based on whims or based on false data. I'm not into fads and just because someone says this has helped them...I must still see if it will help me or my children.

My suggestion would be to take a pill that will contain the essential minerals and vitamins for a day's needs. You may have to do some experimentation in this. Large amounts of any vitamin or mineral need to be taken with caution and probably with your doctor's approval. We have to consider our organs: especially our kidneys and livers, when we are going to take large dosages of ANYTHING! You may be bold enough to take the risk but do you think that you should take on that position when it comes to giving little ones massive dosages of anything that may have long reaching; unproven; and possibly destructive consequences. I cite here the common cold. Would it be wiser to let a cold run its course or dose it with multiple times the recommended dosages of vitamin C or Zinc? Vitamin C is an acid and it has to be filtered by the liver and kidneys. The same can be said for zinc that has to be filtered. How much damage are we doing to our organs when the common cold makes us uncomfortable? I would liken it to killing flies with a .357 magnum!!

Let me also remind you that it is the parent's responsibility to make sure that the children are eating properly and that they are receiving the proper dosages of needed vitamins and minerals. You have the first and final say in what your child eats and drinks. Please educate yourself in the whole area of nutrition and don't dismiss the dangers that are real and are really out there. Parents should want healthy children and we can make the difference.

We spoke earlier of visiting the doctor for emergency situations. If we have good insurance, we may want to also consider periodic checkups.

Periodic checkups should be with a properly licensed pediatrician. We are not telling you to go run to the doctor at the first sign of a cold. We are referring to the different stages of growth that a child normally experiences. One wants to know as soon as possible if a child's growth is abnormal in any of these stages. There are child diseases that will be encountered. You can get a good deal of quality advice by talking with several other parents about how they handled different cases. Compare all of the parents: Do not only listen to the first one you come across.

Again, I am not a doctor and do not represent what I have to say as doctor's advice. Consult doctors for doctor's advice. With that being said, it has been my experience that just good common sense can save a big medical bill. I treat the common cold with bed rest, lots of liquids (**NOT SODA POP!!**) light meals (whatever they can tolerate), and time (more of this than anything else).

Sore throats, on the other hand can be serious. These need to be treated as serious until proven otherwise. To the untrained eye a sore throat is a sore throat. This is not the case.

The untrained eye cannot always determine whether the sore throat is strep or something else which can be considered less threatening. Strep throat should **NEVER BE IGNORED, NOR SHOULD YOU ATTEMPT TO TREAT IT WITH HOME REMEDIES!** Strep only responds to antibiotics. Strep can lead to other more life threatening diseases later in life. Strep throat can, in later years, be blamed for kidney failure, among several other nasty things.

Peace of mind is worth a lot. If a problem persists longer than you feel comfortable, bring the child to the doctor. I hear you...doctor's charges are high and getting higher, but it is still better to be safe than sorry.

Now we deal with another problem which ignorance has produced. Patients have been badgering doctors to write more and more prescriptions for antibiotics. This is the case whether for themselves and/or their children. Much of the general population has become immune to the protective effects of antibiotic treatments.

Antibiotics have been such a wonder treatment for so many years; we think that they will cure anything.

Many diseases and infections have built up immunity to anti—biotics. The continued use of antibiotics for anything and everything is just enlarging the list of things that in which they will become further immune. It is important that we all let our doctors call the shots in this regard. Don't pressure him to do something that he doesn't want to do and you may regret in years to come. Understand this: **ANTIBIOTICS DO NOT KILL THE COMMON COLD GERM (OR VIRUS)!** As of this writing, there are some new and hopeful experiments that seem to do the job. Only if and when they come out might we have a cure for the common cold. Until then anti—biotics are not it.

Anti-biotics can cause "yeast infection" in girls. Yeast infection is a much more long lasting and serious problem stemming from the use of anti—biotics.

A lot of good health is attributed to good hygiene habits. We don't want to created an "obsessive compulsive" type here, but washing of hands is generally a very good habit to develop in a child. Especially is this the case when the child has used the bathroom facilities. Most of this will be learned by example and some teaching.

Many diseases and germs can be stopped in their tracks if everyone would wash their hands. Children, especially, get into things that are not the most sanitary. They also have habits of wiping their noses with the back of their hands and other adult favorites. Just this simple step can reduce the number of colds and other problems of health in your home. Teach it! Practice it!

There is a raging controversy concerning fluoride being added to the public water supply, but statistics are bearing out the fact that this has done more to stop infant and child tooth decay than any other thing within the past two decades. We will not jump on any bandwagon here, but let me say that most tooth decay and other problems **CAN BE PREVENTED!**

The first line of defense is a program of proper tooth brushing and flossing. Again, as with everything else, parents **MUST SET THE EXAMPLE!** Teach your child the proper way to brush and floss his teeth. Next, instill in you child the real and important need to brush and floss his teeth after each and every meal. Get literature that will impress on the child's mind, the very real importance of this simple act.

Bathing (I should say showering in this present age) is also extremely important for several reasons. The first is quite obvious.

We bathe to get the dirt and filth off. The second reason is equally important, even though it may go unknown or unnoticed. We bathe to take the old dead skin away. This helps little growing boys and girls to easily replace the old dead cells and grow new cells. Thirdly, bathing also rids the body of germs and diseases which may have attached themselves to the skin.

After we have gotten these little bodies all clean and smelling good, it is equally necessary to put them in well repaired and clean clothing. Clothing provides modesty, but it also is a defense for minor injuries. The tougher the clothing for little children, the better. That pair of really strong jeans may be the difference between a scraped and bloody knee and just a hurt spot.

Dress for the weather. This does not mean, take your clothes off when it becomes hot and sunny. Just the opposite. Have you ever noticed how the people in hot climates dress? They don't take their clothes off. They wear light and loose fitting clothing. When they sweat and the sweat makes their clothing moist, the wind passing over and through the moist clothing produces a cooling action. A person subjects himself/herself and your children to some very nasty effects from the sun beating down on skin. Sunscreens may have some effect on the cancerous rays of the sun, but they cannot do anything for the cooling effect. In fact, all lotions clog up the skin's pores so that the skin cannot be properly cooled.

In the colder weather you, as the parent, need to make sure that your children are properly dressed. Remember, children are not born with instinct (or common sense). What they may consider proper attire for the winter storms and sub-zero weather may not even come close to what you consider healthy.

As has been seen in so many other areas, parents teach as much by example as by what they say. How will you expect your child to properly dress when you run around scantily clothed during the summer months and with a T-shirt on in the winter? Part of the sacrifice of properly raising your children is that you must always consider your actions and the example that you may be setting. Be sure, the way you act and your visible examples will be the type that is set for your children to duplicate.

Now we address the subject of our immediate environment. We are not talking about the outdoors and whether the "snail darter" will become extinct or not. We are speaking of the inside of your home, your car, the school that your children attend, the church building. These all have an impact on your child's health.

We must instill in our children some good housekeeping habits. Animals must be controlled. Animal hair is a big cause of asthma in some people. Couches and stuffed chairs need to be vacuumed on a regular basis. Even though you may not be able to see the dust and dirt, that does not mean it isn't there.

Carpets are the worst culprits for harboring fugitive bacteria, mites, disease, etc. Carpets need to be cleaned on a regular basis. They need to be vacuumed and shampooed to rid them of some bad critters.

Dirty dishes should not be left in the sink for long periods. They attract cockroaches. If you can cope with it, I would suggest a bit of chlorine bleach in the dishwater.

If you have a central heating and air conditioning unit, make sure that the filters are regularly cleaned and changed. Once a year you should have your air ducts cleaned by a professional.

Bedding harbors mites and other unseen beasties. Launder all bedding on a regular basis and don't be afraid to use bleach on whites or special bleach for colored.

Open as many windows as often as possible. Fresh air is still the best air (unless you live in a polluted area...in which case...**DO NOT EVER OPEN YOUR WINDOWS!!** We will often even keep the windows open (just a crack) in the winter time (especially in the bedrooms). If you follow this advice, make sure that the cold air doesn't affect the plumbing in the house. Usually if you close the door to your bedroom, you won't affect anything else in the house.

Children need fresh air. Open windows in their bedrooms. Give them plenty of blankets and comforters. Encourage them to play out doors when they are able. Play along with them...you need the fresh air also.

We do need to be concerned about our family's health and environment. It is a multifaceted problem. It is the adult's (parents) responsibility. The better informed that you are, the safer your children will be when it comes to good health. We must not take this responsibility lightly. Education is the key to setting the proper environment for good health. Through a program of self education, we will know what to do and when to do it. Education will keep you, the parent, from panicking and/or "freezing up" when the situation calls for decisive and positive action. Education will also keep you from ignoring serious problems. Know what to do and when to do it.

Chapter 4
The Best Bang for the Buck

"Making it," in this day and age, can take some doing. If you are going to be able to raise children on one person's income (the preferred course for child rearing), you are going to need to learn how to be **VERY** resourceful. One must swallow one's pride. It is possible that a parent will be forced into a situation that may attack his/her sense of pride. Perhaps you will have to clothe your children with hand-me-downs or with yard sale specials. It's also quite possible that you may be driving a used (not new) and not so pretty car. There are times when you will need to cook lesser cuts of meat.

I'll guarantee you that if you let pride get in the way it will cost you, in a very big way, in dollars and cents. We want to try to do the best thing for our children. It is possible that the best thing for them is not what they want, but what the child needs the most. If we try to provide everything new, we will either not be able to provide everything that the child needs, or, we will sink ourselves so deeply in debt that we will not be able to act responsibly, as a Christian and a good steward of what God has allowed us to have.

The first line of defense is to set priorities. Both parents need to sit down, together, and decide what is most demanding of our limited capital. We will be asking ourselves some questions, such as: Must we have the newest and the best, or would second hand and/or used be just as functional? What priorities are we going to set on spiritual things such as rallies and church events? There will be secular activities in which we could involve ourselves. Then we need to consider just how involved, (financially speaking) we will be in birthday parties, holidays, vacations, and other events and celebrations.

Our second line of defense against inflation and the shrinking dollar would be involvement in the national pastime called "YARD SALEING". Even though this has become a new sport, it can also be a great way to stretch the budget. If you are going to help the budget and not hurt the budget, there are some major rules that you must keep in mind.

Rule number one: **GO WITH A WELL THOUGHT OUT LIST OF WHAT YOU REALLY NEED!** One should not shop for food when they are hungry **AND**...one must not go shopping at garage sales like a child in a candy store. You will be amazed at what you think you "**NEED**" when you see what is available. A list will keep you on track as for why you are really there.

Yard sales can give you needed items at a small fraction of the cost that you would pay for the same items from the mall or from some chain discount stores. The problem arises, however, (when we are not careful) in that we make up for all the money that we have saved by ignoring our priority list and just purchasing someone else's junk.

The second rule for yard sale shopping is this: **KNOW EVERYONE'S VITAL STATISTICS SUCH AS SIZE, COLOR PREFERENCES, ETC..** It's bad enough that you may not have every member of the family with you when you go yard sale shopping: don't exacerbate the problem by your ignorance of all their vital stats.

It would behoove you to also know the ranges of sizes. Is a neck size of 16 considered small, medium, or large? How do dress sizes interrelate? What size does "petite" translate into? Know if the person can wear a size 9 1/2 D **AND** a size 10B. You may have to have enough savvy to understand that a size 10 in one brand may not be the same as a size 10 in some other brand. There is nothing worse than getting home only to find out that the thing that you paid good money for, **DOESN'T FIT**. There are no refunds or returns with yard sale purchases…you have just lost money trying to save money. The only alternative to any of this is to have every member of the family equipped with a cell phone (and you know each and every number and to whom it belongs).

The third rule for garage sales is this: **IF IN DOUBT...DO NOT BUY IT!!!!** We often think, "Oh well, it's only a dollar." Only a dollar here and only a dollar there can add up to a pair of shoes somewhere else or it could be the shirt that you weren't able to buy. If you are not sure of the size or you don't know if the item will be accepted by the person that it is intended for, just don't take the chance. There will be other garage sales and other items that may not be exactly the same, but will be similar enough to fill the need.

Now we come to a very tricky, but often effective means of stretching the old buck. Auctions. Auctions can be dangerous if you don't really know what you are doing. There is a certain amount of excitement and emotions that drive the bidding. As with the garage sales, set down and adhere to a list of rules governing auctions.

Rule number one: **MAKE A LIST OF WHAT YOU REALLY NEED AND LOOKING FOR.** Same rule that we had with the garage sales. A "need" can be generated in the excitement of the bidding. If you don't go with the list, you will come back with something that you may regret buying.

Rule number two: **SET A LIMIT...(BEFORE THE BIDDING STARTS)...OF HOW MUCH YOU ARE WILLING TO PAY FOR AN ITEM.** Pray about it. If you can't pray, you can't pay. Know and realize that you can get carried away.

Rule number three: **ALWAYS HAVE ANOTHER RESPONSIBLE PERSON WITH YOU (PREFERABLY YOUR HUSBAND OR YOUR WIFE) TO KEEP YOU "HONEST".** There is nothing like a wife to "pour cold water" all over your extravagant dreams. Your mate can become a "reality check" for you. Questions such as, "Honey, what are you going to do with that thing when you get it home?...or..."How did we ever get along without one of those all these years"? These may not go far in being warm and fuzzy, but it may bring us to our senses.

Rule number four: **PICTURE YOURSELF CARRYING THIS THING HOME.** I say this because you may have to carry it home. How will it fit in the trunk? Everyone doesn't have a pickup truck and some of us don't even have access to a pickup truck. Be very realistic about what you are buying and how you are going to transport it.

Now we come to the idea of a "thrift store". These may fly under different categories, but they are really "thrift stores". The thrift store can carry many different products on its shelves. Some of these are run by not-for-profit organizations. Some of them are run to make a profit. Each of them has its own unique advantages and disadvantages. There are thrifts for baked goods; "salvage groceries"; furniture and appliances; used books; clothing; multiple lines of products. You can be sure that all of these thrift stores can save you money if you shop wisely. The best way to use these stores to your greatest advantage is to keep your "ear to the ground" and know just what is available. Again, you will only be able to take advantage of the thrift stores great savings if you are not a slave to personal pride.

Let us deal with the clothing thrifts. Usually, unlike the yard sale, there is little or no "negotiating". The advantage of the clothing thrift, however, is that it is open during "regular hours". The pressure to, "buy it now or the next person will get it", is not so great. There is also usually a greater selection of merchandise available. The chances of finding the sizes that you are looking for are much greater. Shopping the thrift allows you to buy high quality items for "pennies on the dollar".

A decided disadvantage with the thrift store is that prices are usually higher than your average yard sale. Unlike the yard sale, however, you can usually take things back (even if it's only to swap). Clothing thrifts also have another advantage over the yard sale in that you can usually try on the clothes that you are thinking of buying. This can be a special advantage if you have a hard-to-fit person in the family.

The next form of thrift is the bakery thrift. Here you will be able to get "day old" baked goods at a greatly reduced price. Most baked goods have so much preservative in them that they are quite capable of staying "fresh" for many days beyond your purchase date. Most bakery thrifts are very careful to make sure that the items that they place out for purchase have plenty of "shelf life" in them. To be safe, however, it might be a good idea for you to check them out, as well.

Look for mold in baked goods. Sometimes you will not be able to see it and you may, from time-to-time, buy one or two items that are really not fit to eat! Look at the expiration date on the wrappers. You will learn which things will usually survive long after that date and which ones will stick close to that expiration time.

If you should be so blessed that there are more than one baked good thrifts in your area, visit them all. There can be a real difference in pricing from one to another. Also one company may have "fresher" goods than its competition. Look for sales on baked goods. These also will differ from one store to the next.

Salvage goods thrift stores can cut your grocery bills in half. There is some risk to buying "jammed cans", but you can educate yourself in what to look for. The employees in the store would be more than happy teach you the heads up rules for buying surplus groceries. Some rules that I have learned over the years: If the can is broken anywhere...don't eat. If the can sends a stream of liquid way up when opened, don't eat. If, when you press on the end of a can and it makes a "popping noise", don't eat it.

For the most part the store employees will look each and every can over pretty good before they will allow them to reach the shelves. When in doubt...throw it out.

One would want to be careful about purchasing packages that have burst open. These usually don't make it to the shelves, but sometimes they may slip by. A lot of your decisions will be made easier if you only shop at surplus food stores that have a good reputation.

Some food thrifts also will sell refrigerated items. Generally it is safe to purchase these items. All cities and states that I am familiar with have stringent health laws which apply equally to regular grocery stores and to "salvage groceries" thrift stores. Be very careful with meat. Look the meat over well and make sure there is no mold growing on it. Again, I cannot stress enough the need to shop stores with good reputations. Some salvage stores will sell brand new merchandise along with salvage groceries. The new products will be well marked. If in doubt ask an employee.

Furniture and appliances can also be purchased at thrift stores. The savings here can be tremendous. Look over the item well before you purchase it. If you are buying an appliance, **ALWAYS SEE, HEAR, AND EXPERIENCE THIS APPLIANCE RUNNING.** If you are not allowed to do this...**DON'T BUY THE APPLIANCE!!**

Perhaps these cannot be truly classified as a "thrift store", but I have seen great deals in places that sell used tires. Sometimes these places are found at your friendly neighborhood auto salvage lot (junk yards). In many cases, used tires are sold exclusively in a used tire store. Again, reputation should weigh very heavily in which place to frequent. You need to inspect the tire **CLOSELY** before you buy.

The best places are those that give some kind of a guarantee, even if that guarantee is that they will replace any defective tire that you return with another tire of equal value and quality. Generally you won't realistically be able to expect a mileage guarantee on a used tire unless you are paying "top dollar" for an almost new tire.

In the same area, let us address the auto salvage lot (junk yard). There are times when buying from a salvage lot could be O.K.. Some people will **NEVER** buy from a salvage lot. I probably will not change your mind. I would, however, purchase used auto parts from a salvage lot if certain criteria were in place: 1. I would have to save at least fifty percent (50%) over that same part, new, from a auto supply store. 2. I would have to determine (guesswork) that the used part would last as long as the car I'm putting it into.

3. If, at all possible, I would like to get a part from a car that is actually newer than the car I am placing that part into. For instance, many parts are made to cover several year models of that particular car (interchangeable parts). If, for example, I have a 1999 Ford Escort and I need a brake caliper, Ford may have made the same caliper for all Escorts from 1996 until they stopped building Escorts. I would want my part to be from a car that was close to the last one made. This could mean more mileage to expect from the part and lesser wear and tear than the same part from a 1999 Ford Escort. 4. I would never by a wearable part from a salvage yard. Wearable parts are things, such as, hoses, belts, brake pads, etc..

A thrift store can certainly save you a great deal of money. As with anything else that is used, however, buyers DO need to be wary. I have not listed all of the possible type stores that exist. Keep a sharp eye out for other typos of stores that can save you money. Also shop thrift stores of the same kind to get the best prices and quality. If you are really very careful, you can cut your budget well in half in these different areas, if you will buy used or salvage, over new.

Before I get completely off of the thrift stores, I have another store in mind that isn't usually thought of as a "thrift store". Pawn shops have some very good deals. You must be convicted of the fact that the person getting the money for the object was better off by pawning that item in the first place. If you feel guilty buying pawned items, DON'T DO IT!

Also "meat lockers" can really save you a lot on frozen products...especially meats. If you have some property, you could raise two pigs or two cows, etc., and use one to pay for the processing of the other. Everyone wins and you can be assured of the quality of the meat that you personally raised. Sometimes also, meat lockers will sell at the owner's option, some of his meat to the public at a reduced price.

Finally, let me say that we live in a society in which prices are named and, in general, no bartering is allowed. It is not this way in most of the civilized world. In most countries and in many societies, people will "gladly negotiate" (the polite word) the price of an item. In our own country, we do this with cars and houses and a few other items (mostly "big ticket" items). The truth is, however, if you can actually speak to an owner respectfully and expectantly, you may find that he/she is open to some "negotiating". Most of your success in these kinds of deals, heavily rests upon the way that you approach the owner. If you expect to intimidate (bully) this owner into dropping price, you can forget any chance for negotiations. Most prices can be made negotiable, but some rules always need to be heeded.

Never be insulting or rude in any way! You are really looking for a favor from this owner. Most owners do not take kindly to people who insult their products. You might, instead, start your conversation by building up the product and the company. Then after you have built value into their product, you might approach the owner from the standpoint of, "This is such a great product. In fact it is so wonderful; I don't think that I could ever expect you to lower its price". Whether you say these words out loud, or not, this is the idea that you want to get across.

This opens things up to the owner trying to find out if you would buy it if the price were a little lower. If he takes the bait, negotiations are under way. Always conduct yourself with respect and honor. You do not have to be rude to negotiate a better price on an item. This is where so many people mess up and actually lose the advantage. Remember, the owner doesn't need to drop his price. He will be best persuaded to drop his price if he likes and respects you, not, if he can't stand you because of your abrasive manners.

We also need to be realistic in what we expect to save from the listed price. If the owner is only marking the product up by thirty percent, you would not be realistic in wanting him to cut his profit by twenty percent. If he operated this way, he would not long stay in business.

When I was in auto sales, one of the short cuts to negotiations would be when either the customer or I would declare what we would like to see the owner make as a profit. I might say to the customer, "Would you think it fair that the dealership maybe makes a profit of one thousand dollars on this nineteen thousand dollar car?" The customer would then assent or dissent to this number and make a counter offer. Realism dictates that if there is an owner and we are **NOT** a not-for-profit business, then making a profit should not be viewed as some kind of sin.

The negotiations are to determine with what figure the owner and the customer would both be comfortable

In this entire chapter, I would be remiss in not considering this aspect of buying smart. What does God think of all this? We, as Christians need to keep God in the picture. There is absolutely nothing wrong with taking the time to pray before you make a purchase. Many times something or someone is pressuring us to make snap decisions. Let this little rule become a controlling part of your life: **WHENEVER I AM PRESSED TO MAKE A DECISION QUICKLY...I WON'T MAKE THAT DECISION AT ALL UNTIL AT LEAST TWENTY FOUR HOURS HAVE PASSED.** In this time, you can consult God and meditate on the wisdom of the decision that is being called for. Car sales managers, and salesmen **HATE THIS.** Do not let them control the situation..........**YOU CONTROL IT!** Even if someone else will buy the car out from under you. They probably won't, but even if they do...you can **KNOW** that God helped make this decision.

Again, If what you were interested in is gone, take this as a message (answer to prayer) that God does not want you to have this now. Rejoice and praise God for His real interest in what you were so confused about.

This practice is very very hard for people of an impatient nature. Impetuous purchasing is **NEVER GOOD STEWARDSHIP!** This is very hard for people who are used to getting what they want (and when they want it). This may be the case for the people of the world. They feel that they control their own destinies and that they "make their own "luck". Christians, on the other hand, understand all too well that if God is not in it, then we labor (and purchase) in vain **(Psalm 127:1)**

In conjunction with prayer, ask yourself, "Do I really NEED this, or is this just a 'want'". When we think about it with our heads clear and without any emotion or pressure, we come to the realization that we have simply stimulated a desire for something.

We need to consider the "Big Picture" when we are contemplating a purchase. All purchases will affect our budget and our Christian Stewardship! All purchases will create a negative cash flow. All purchases will demand more time at work or less money for other things which may be 'TRUE NEEDS"!

If you are going to survive and raise children and stay on a one wage earner income, you are going to need to have a plan in regards to spending money.

As frugal as you may be, no amount of yard sales or thrift stores will be able to control you spending habits. If you do not control those spending habits, your spending habits will control you.

A good budget will need to be customized, but ANY budget should include at least the following: 1. A tithe of AT LEAST TEN PERCENT (or whatever you believe should be given to support the Church on Earth. Remember, a physical "church" needs physical finances to continue to operate and meet your physical needs.) 2. Housing expenses (rent, or mortgage payment). 3. Utilities (gas, electric, telephone, water, etc., etc. 4. Food. 5. Work lunches (brown bag, eating out [not recommended]. 6. Toiletries. 7. Allowances (both for children and for adults). 8. Barber and beauty shop. 9. Gasoline, oil (misc. car needs). 10. Car repairs/tires/tags, etc. 11. Insurances (life, auto, health). 12. Medical expenses (dental, prescriptions, uncovered medical expense, health insurance payments). 13. Automobile payment. 14. Clothing. 15. Dry cleaning/laundry (suggest that you get a washer and dryer if you don't already have one. 16. Gifts. 17. Periodicals (newspaper, magazines, books, etc.). 18. Vacation. 19. Savings. 20. Entertainment (eating out, sporting events, concerts, etc.). 21. Child care expenses (baby sitting from time-to time). 22. Credit card payments (which probably shouldn't have been generated to begin with [**DO NOT PAY JUST THE MINIMUM PAYMENT OR I WILL PERSONALLY COME TO YOUR HOME WITH A SANDWICH BOARD SAYING** "The person who lives in this house is from outer space"]) 23. Whatever expenses are incurred in heating and air conditioning your home (no "fudging"). 24. Miscellaneous (and there will be some miscellaneous).

Even though these expenses need to be considered on a monthly basis, they need to also be planned for on an annual basis, as well. For instance, clothing: You may not need to purchase any clothing for several months in a row, but along comes the opening of school and you now have to spend **HUN-**

DREDS OF DOLLARS ON SCHOOL CLOTHING. If you have not made plans for this, you will bankrupt the budget. If, on the other hand, you have figured your annual clothing expenses (from looking in last year's expenditures on clothing and have set aside the amount of $681.55 {the amount that you spent last year for school things}. And you had this all figured out and taken care of in June) you then will be thought the best financial guru around!!

Even beyond this cleverness, you have divided this sum into 12 small payments of 56.71 (which is 1 twelfth of 681.55) for next year's school shopping. You will probably be put in Time magazine. Now, when school time comes around, you will not have to apply for a signature loan to pay for all of this mess.

You may be able to be a little frugal and cut costs of utility bills by an appreciable amount. For instance: sleep with extra blankets or under several quilts or better yet, sleep with an electric blanket and turn the heat down. (Careful that you don't allow pipes to freeze). Encourage everyone to wear sweaters and other warm clothing when lounging about, in the winter months.

Miscellaneous also needs to be a generous box to fill. Some use the savings as a miscellaneous. Either way, you need to plan for the unplanable. One of Murphy's laws should be, "Be sure that whatever you don't expect to happen, will".

As clever as we are, there is always room for more input from others. Ask around and look around, you will pick up something of value from those in which you are in daily contact. It may be something useful that you can do with your empty milk jugs, or it may be something that you can substitute in your cooking that would be less expensive than what you usually use. If you don't ask, most often you won't receive. Look at it this way: if you just did something very clever or did something that would save you money, would you go around telling everybody? Of course not. This would be considered "tooting your own horn". Don't expect everyone to volunteer all of the useful things that they have done. On the other hand, if you have done something really clever and someone asks you a question concerning it, would you let them in on the secret? Again, of course you would. Ask, and you shall receive doesn't just apply to the spiritual things of life.

We need to be wise as serpents if we expect to survive with children and only one person working outside the home. A paycheck can only stretch so far. Remember, in all of this your best protection against disaster is to keep the Lord, your God in the picture.

It has been said and bears repeating (concerning the practice of "tithing"), "The Lord can do more for you with ninety percent than you can do for yourself with one hundred percent". The same principle carries through in every aspect of our lives. With us the situation may seem impossible; but always remember, with God, **ALL THINGS ARE POSSIBLE.** If God be with us and for us, who or what can be against us?

Chapter 5
Discipline

Discipline:
1. A branch of knowledge or learning.
2. Training that develops self-control, Character, or orderliness and efficiency.
3. The result of such training; self-control; orderly conduct.
4. Acceptance of, or submission to, authority and control.
5. A system of rules or methods, as for the conduct of members of a monastic order.
6. Treatment that corrects or punishes.
(Webster)

You will notice that the LAST definition is the one that most people think of first. Discipline is not one and the same as corporal punishment but it is so often thought of as one and the same. Discipline is a teaching and a training method. Corporal punishment is part of discipline, but discipline is not limited to corporal punishment.

When is the right time to use corporal punishment (spanking)? Children have been spanked for many things that either they have no control over, or they did not understand the error of their actions. Sometimes it simply boils down to a judgment call. I know that some have tried to put this down to a scientific formula of sorts. According to them, any time a child says "no" they should be spanked. I firmly agree with this, but there are times when a child is in rebellion even though he doesn't portray it. Mom has told the child that is being potty trained to tell her if he needs to go to the bathroom. The next thing you know, the training pants are full at first we could chalk this up to forgetfulness, but after a while it has to be re-evaluated as possibly laziness or outright stubbornness (rebellion). Mom (or Dad) is going to have to make this judgment call. As long as you don't spank as a "knee jerk" reaction, you'll probably be just fine.

Parents will make mistakes and possibly spank a child when the child was not truly deserving of it, but don't fret too much about it. The child will not hold that against you. That child knows perfectly well how many times he did something wrong and **DIDN'T** receive a spanking for it.

We will deal a lot with corporal punishment in this chapter because it seems to be the form of punishment that is so often misunderstood and/or misused. I want to deal with **WHEN** (which I have already pretty much covered to some extent) and we need to deal with **HOW**. Understand that it's not as I did on a regular basis, but what I learned from my mistakes which I share with you. You might be saying, "I know how to spank my child"!! Perhaps you do, but so many people do not know **HOW** to mete out corporal punishment. To properly cover the subject, we will go back to "square one".

"Square one": You must lay down the rules and make sure that your child understands these rules. You cannot just start spanking because something you child is doing bothers you. If you have not already sat you child(ren) down and explained that this particular behavior is wrong and is not going to be tolerated, you **MUST NOT SPANK THEM** the first time that this offensive behavior is displayed. This is the time for the explanations and the warning. You must tell them **EXACTLY WHAT BEHAVIOR YOU EXPECT FROM HIM (THEM)**. Have the child(ren) repeat back to you what you are trying to get across. After you are satisfied that the child understands what you are pointing our, you need to set the penalty for the offense (in this portion of the chapter, we will be speaking of spanking, but we will also cover other penalties). "Sammy", if you pull the dog's tail again I will spank you. Now, Sammy, repeat back to me what you understand that I just said". When Sammy gets it straight, he is now on notice that a spanking is awaiting him if he pulls the pet's tail. **YOU MUST SPANK THIS CHILD IF HE PULLS THE DOG'S TAIL AGAIN. NEVER** make a rule and go back on the enforcement of that rule. **THE ENFORCEMENT MUST BE JUST EXACTLY WHAT YOU PROMISED!!**

Never shout at Sammy when he pulls the dog's tail and then spank him. Shouting is not a trait that you want to cultivate in yourself, nor do you want to teach your child secondary lessons, such as: Mom or Dad only really mean it if they shout...or...It's O.K. to shout, Mom and Dad do. You will end up with a whole family of "shouters". Just lead the child into a private room and spank him/her there.

I cannot begin to tell you just how important it is to not shout. You will open a "Pandora's box" of problems when you allow yourself or your child to raise his/her voice. You may intimidate the child the first few times and this may embolden you to continue on the course...DON'T! The effect that you like (getting the child's attention) will soon wear off and you will, in the end, realize just the opposite effect.

Closely related to the shouting, when it comes to the realm of conditioned stimulus and responses: "Is it going to need repeating every time". When you ask (or tell) your child to do something they need to do it. AND NOW. There should be no need to repeat yourself (unless they really did not hear you). Again, however, you must set the "ground rules" and have them repeat the "ground rules" back to you. Next you must establish the penalty for not responding...IN A TIMELY MANNER.

I can tell you from first hand knowledge that children will test you in these areas, over-and-over-again! When I was a young man (in my early teen years) my job on Saturday was to take out the garbage and to clean the house. I can remember one Saturday quite well. It was the Saturday that I learned to ignore my mother. I had done the cleaning of the house and I was sitting down to rest. My rest took a little longer than was acceptable and my mother told me to take out the garbage. I was almost ready to hop up and do it when a "brain-storm" struck. I decided to purposely test my mother. I simply stayed where I was. Mother shouted a little louder. I stayed right where I was. Two or three minutes passed by. Mother shouted again. I KNEW THAT I HAD WON. After about four calls, each of them being a little louder, she finally said, "Oh never mind, I'll just do it myself". AND SHE DID!!

Repetitive requests and shouting go hand in hand. Some rules that parents need to impose upon themselves are: Never raise your voice and do not be lead into the trap of repeating yourself. You need to discipline after the first infraction.

This leads me to another rule for parents. Do not spank in public (if you can help it). Don't do it at Church; don't do it at home; don't do it anywhere in public. This is not to become a public spectacle. You are attempting to train the child with this spanking. You should not be attempting to disgrace, embarrass, and degrade your child in front of his/her peers, or worse yet…in front of total strangers or adult members of the congregation that the child cares for. You **MUST** take the child away into a private place.

There is another good reason to discipline your child in private. You should go over the rule(s) that he/she just broken. Make sure that they know why they are getting a spanking. If they don't know why, they are going to build up resentment towards you. Also, if they do not know why, you will not be training them to **NOT** do that offensive behavior again.

You are not spanking your child because they have upset you. You are spanking your child to train them (by the use of "negative stimulus", not to repeat actions that are socially unacceptable. You are training them to blend in with society and behave properly. If you follow the previously stated rules consistently, you will not need to pay much attention to the next paragraph.

NEVER SPANK YOUR CHILD IN ANGER ! ! ! EVEN IF THE INFRACTION WARRANTS A SPANKING. Anger sends all of the wrong messages. Angry spankers send the message that they are angry and the child must not make them angry. You say, "Fine, that IS the message that I want them to understand". No you don't…You want your child to understand that he/she has broken a well defined rule. Spanking should **NEVER** be a vent to your anger and hostility.

When that child grows a little older, he will vent his hostilities in the same way as he has been taught. It is quite possible (and has happened multiple times) that your child will turn around and beat **YOU** up. You are not there to build bitterness and hostility in your child; you are there to **T R A I N** that child(ren) to be a proper sociable human being(s).

If you ever are about to spank your child in anger, **S T O P !** Do not even spank that child at all, while you are in that frame of mind. Get a grip on your emotions. This whole process may take a great deal of time. You may regain control in five minutes, or it may take you a day. Make sure that the child knows that you have to gain control of your own emotions. This will help the child understand why he/she is not receiving the spanking that he/she so richly deserves. When you are completely calm and back in control, take your child aside and explain to him/her that he/she has done something deserving of a spanking, but that he/she has caused Mommy or Daddy to become so angry that you cannot spank him/her at this time. Reassert the rule and the punishment and let your child know that he/she **WILL** receive a spanking the next time the he/she does the unacceptable behavior.

So much of the time corporal punishment is not really necessary. On some children, corporal punishment is **NOT** the best form of discipline.

Some children will dig in their heels and refuse to let you "get to them" with a spanking. I have heard some say that they would just "spank it out of them". Folks, I want you to know that there is such a thing as **CHILD ABUSE**. If the spanking routine does not work, you **MUST NOT BEAT THE CHILD!!** There are alternatives to corporal punishment. Some of these are as effective as or even more effective than corporal punishment...**IF USED PROPERLY!**

I like to call this "creative discipline". You can't be lazy or unthinking when it comes to creative discipline. You must know your child enough to know what he/she likes and/or dislikes. It is those likes and dislikes that you will capitalize on.

I had a child that would not respond to spankings. She loved to run around with the other children. She was a great big ball of energy and was always into things. After failure in the regular ways of corporal punishment, I determined to discipline her with some "creative discipline". I would place a chair in the middle of the room and make her sit there. She was not allowed to talk to anyone or her time would double. She could not play or in any way interact with her siblings. I would not even let her play with her own hands. She thought this was so much fun...at first. After about fifteen minutes or so, she asked if she could get up. I ALWAYS SAID NO! I told her to think about the wrong thing that she had done. She asked me again a little later,

Again I said no. It wasn't until she began to cry that I started to time her for fifteen minutes before I would let her up. She got the message, LOUD AND CLEAR!

There are many forms of "creative discipline" that can be just as effective. You must fit the punishment to the deed and especially to the child. To start your thinking on different items of creative discipline, I offer the following list. Remember, this list is not exhaustive and may not be the best for your child. Also remember, you must get to the child with something that he/she really likes or really hates. Here is the list: 1. Take away phone privileges. 2. Don't let the child play with friends for a specified time (remember, you want to make it hurt for them to get the point). 3. No sweets for a week. 4. Here's one that worked on one of my children... Only three meals a day AND ABSOLUTELY NO IN BETWEEN SNACKS! (She was counting the hours until the restriction was lifted). 5. No going to any stores for a specified period of time. 6. Make them hoe portions of the garden. I think that you get the idea. Be creative...help them understand the point of correction.

Whatever the child **LIKES** or whatever the child **DISLIKES** is what will be the most effective lever. Remember, do not really even think of starting the appropriate time period **UNTIL THE CHILD STARTS CRYING** or in some other way is letting you know that you have his/her undivided attention. Remind him of what he has done and why he is receiving this punishment. Even in this, you can abuse a child. Make sure you are not venting a sadistic tendency in seeing the child "pay for getting you upset".

Be consistent in whatever form of punishment you mete out. Consistency covers a lot of ground. You need to do what you tell them you are going to do. Do not spank one time and use creative discipline the next time for the same offense (unless you have discussed the change in between occurrences with the child). Do not discipline one time and ignore the same offense the next time. Do not discipline one child for an offense and let another child get away with impunity while doing the same misdeed. Children have a very good grasp of "**FAIRNESS**". You must be even handed when you mete out punishment.

You must also be consistent, as a team. It is certainly preferable for both parents to agree on the discipline to be used. This is not always the case, however. My wife and I were married before we became Christians and before we saw the real need to discuss child discipline. Later, when we had children and wanted to do the right thing by them, as Christians, we found that we were on opposite poles. Neither one of us was willing to compromise our position and this made things very difficult. Christian parents **MUST** compromise on things that are not a matter of salvation or you will go through some extreme discipline problems. I speak from experience; settle on the discipline principles **BEFORE** you get married, if at all possible!! If this does not happen, each parent **MUST** be consistent in his or her form of discipline. Never should one parent openly criticize (by word or action) the discipline that the other parent has used. In private these differences can (and should) be discussed, but it should not happen in front of the children.

Also, if Dad practices "creative discipline", he would greatly confuse his children if he decided to spank for some particular offense without any discussion of the change in discipline from him. Usually this happens when Dad gets **REALLY MAD**. We have already touched on this earlier in this chapter. If you are spanking because you are angry, you are abusing your power as a parent.

In a somewhat related subject, make sure that you always attempt to fit the punishment to the crime. This can only be done if and when you can calm down and think properly. Too great a punishment and you will embitter your child. On the other hand, if the punishment is not great enough, you defeat the whole purpose of punishment.

The point will not be made and the child will not fear the repercussions of his/her actions. It has been my observation that most parents don't give too little punishment. I have observed, on many occasions, that the parent has overburdened the child with too great of a punishment. I have also observed a great deal of bitterness in the youth of today and I believe that some of it certainly stems from this factor.

Remember, parents, just enough to get the point across. This is not a time to take out your anger and frustration on the child. It is not a time to become sadistic and vindictive. **YOU SHOULD BE DISCIPLINING SO THAT YOUR CHILD WILL LEARN PROPER BEHAVIOR AND RESPONSES IN LIFE.** Any thing else is improper discipline.

Another part of discipline which we have touched on earlier (when we discussed shouting) is the word **NO**. Children must understand that the word, "no", must be respected and obeyed. There are some things that the parent must also understand when using this word. The word "no" is sometimes the lazy parent's way of responding. The child can barely get the request out of his/her mouth and the parent has responded with his deadly six shooter which is loaded with all "no's". We as parents have a very bad tendency of shooting from the hip.

There are reasons for this. Sometimes a parent will habitually respond with "no" because they are afraid to make a decision. Perhaps they use the word "no" because they are fearful of what might happen to their children. Here we are addressing unreasonable fears. Perhaps a parent uses the word "no" to "show just who is in charge".

The word "no" should not be used lightly. Choose your battles. Use the word when it is most appropriate. As "knee jerk" spanking is wrong, so is the "knee jerk **NO**". If you use the word inappropriately, you will do several things to your child. First, you discourage your child. They will start to think that you don't want them to do anything.

If decisions come hard for you, simply tell your child that you will have to think about it. If you tell the child this, **THEN THINK ABOUT IT** and come back with an answer...SOON!! You will be lying to your child if you simply tell Him/them that you want to think about it to get them "off your back".

If you find yourself saying no because of unreasonable fears, you need to seek some help. Your minister, or possibly parents who have successfully raised a good family, probably could do a good job at helping you dispel these fears. Don't penalize your child(ren) with your insecurities. There is a good chance, also, that you will directly or indirectly pass on these fears to your child(ren). The problem will then pass from one generation to another. Help to break this cycle.

Do not play "parental ping-pong". This happens when one parent sends the child to the other parent for **THEM** to make a decision. This is to escape the responsibility of one of the two parents to not have to make this decision. This is not fair to your own loving partner. It is permissible to say, "It's O.K. with me, but it must also be O.K. with your mother/father. Children know who the "soft touch" is, and they will attempt to play one against the other. Do not let them play this game. If you are the "soft touch" you know it. Change your ways of participation in the decision making process. Make sure that both you and your spouse are on the very same page.

We will deal with submission, in depth, at a later time in this book, but I do want to mention it here, as well. Discipline teaches one other lesson to the child. It is a lesson that I don't think many parents of the past have done a good job of getting across. I say that because I believe that this is one of the major problems that confront us in the Church; in our marriages; and in our society, at large. The subject of my concern and one of the goals of discipline is submission. Children **MUST LEARN TO SUBMIT**

TO AUTHORITY. I f they are not taught the lesson, and taught the lesson **WELL** , they will have serious future problems with their bosses; their spouse; the minister; the police; and any other authority figure that they may encounter in life.

The facts of life demand submission, at all levels. You, as a parent, have an important responsibility to instill this characteristic in your children. You do this by the use of discipline and personal example. Your child needs to learn to obey you and place himself/herself under you authority. I cannot begin to impress upon you, as parents, what a critical responsibility you have in this area.

Furthermore, if you do not teach submission at an early age, you will be tormented by your child all the way through the teen years. Even when you do your best, you will be tested when that child reaches ages between fourteen and eighteen. You, as a parent want to lay the groundwork now for a smooth transition from child to young adult. Submission is the brickwork and the foundation for everything else that is brought into that child's life.

In the beginning of this chapter, the definition of discipline was presented,. In that definition we see that one of the purposes of discipline is to teach the child "self control" (something that many adults don't display).

I want to take just a moment to remind all parents that this is one of the reasons for everything that we have discussed up until this time. There should come a time in each child's life when he/she will stop self from doing something wrong or will force self to do that which is right. You have gained the victory when this happens.

You should also reinforce this sense of accomplishment and victory in the child. It does not matter at what age this happens. Teens need reinforcement as much as your little five year old does.

Instilling self control in the child should be your goal as a parent. This should be one of the reasons that you would spank your child; why you wrack your brain for some "creative discipline" methods; why you say and enforce the word, "no"; in short, it is one of the main reasons that you do all that you do as a parent.

Chapter 6
Time Management

There are only twenty four hours in a day. Twenty four hours sounds like a lot of time, and it would be a lot of time, if you only had one thing to do in this block of time. Things such as housework, going shopping, possibly planning out a Sunday school class, going for a walk (for exercise), talking to others on the phone, etc., etc., etc.. How you have planned out your day and the use of these limited amount of hours, will determine just how successful you will be in the proper upbringing of your children.

Let us start by writing out a schedule. In this schedule, you want to include **EVERYTHING** that must be accomplished. I look at this as a type of budget. We budget our money (or we had better budget our money), time is much more valuable and much more limited. If you don't have enough money, there is an undesirable option of getting a second job or the other marriage partner working some kind of a part time job. **NEITHER ONE OF THESE ARE RECOMMENDED OPTIONS.** I bring this up simply out of comparison. If you don't have enough time in the day to get things done, you cannot go out and borrow some...you can't earn some extra time...no, you are given **ONLY** twenty four hours in the day. Use them very wisely. Know what you have to do and plan carefully.

Your time budget should be organized. You can plan your time on a day-to-day basis. Hand to mouth, so to speak. I do not recommend this any more than I would recommend that you plan on how to spend your money on a day-to-day basis.

The shortest plan should be a weekly plan. Each day of the week will be planned out and included in the whole scheme of things for that week. This is probably the best plan. It might be possible to plan for a month, but so many factors can pop up and disrupt your plan in the course of a month. I will not even try to deal with planning your time out in monthly chunks. If you think that you can and want to, simply extend the concept of the weekly plan. Let me say, however, that you should be aware of some things that may be happening in the month. Things like birthdays, anniversaries, Christmas, Thanksgiving, and the like will possibly have an effect on your plans weeks before the event (such as shopping for presents).

Some things can be put in place every day. Things such as meals, cleaning the house, perhaps washing (depending on the size of the family), etc...It would be very hard to change these things around. It might be possible to "adjust" one of these things on an "as needed" basis, but for all intents and purposes, these things remain the same from day to day. It's the things that don't remain the same every day that will wipe you out. Think hard and carefully. Try to recollect all of the things that you need to do today, tomorrow, etc...

Visualize yourself walking through the day. Go from job to job, hour by hour. See yourself, in you mind's eye, doing what needs to be done. The farther you get away from the present, the harder it will be to plan and visualize. Also, the farther you move from the present, the more chance that something will come up that you don't know about, and of course because you don't know about it, you haven't made any plans to deal with it, yet.

In a monetary budget, we make a category labeled, miscellaneous. In you time management budget, it would be hard but you might leave an "unplanned-for" chunk of time for such contingencies. If nothing comes up in that time period, use it for whatever you want to do (or not do).

PRIORITIZE: Select the things that MUST be done or the roof will fall in. Separate these things from the "it would be nice if" things. When you do this, you might find out that because of the restrictions of time, you will not be able to do everything that you would like to do today. Some things might be able to be extended to another day. Some things, however, may not be able to be extended to any other day (birthday parties, concerts, etc..). This is the very reason that you must prioritize. If you fail to do a good job of prioritizing, you will be caught in the vise of having to leave out something very important (perhaps of **FORGETTING** something very important). If you do the job right, those things that are inconsequential will be the things to go by the wayside.

One way to help you remember all the things that have to be planned for is to keep a note list somewhere. Keep several lists if you have to; just get them all together when you are planning your week. **WHENEVER YOU THINK OF SOMETHING WRITE IT DOWN...DO NOT DEPEND ON YOUR MEMORY!!**

Get one of those calendars that have a big square for each day of the week. Make reminder notes in each proper square and refer to this calendar every day. Keep several lists or notes if you have to. If you go for multiple lists, however, you may forget one when you're making your plans. It's best to have only one reference list. No matter when, whenever you think of something, **WRITE IT DOWN** and make sure to transfer it to the master list as soon as possible. **DO NOT DEPEND UPON YOUR MEMORY!!!**

Now you can ignore all that has been written up to this point (and, truth be known this is probably how you may have been running your life up to now), and just live from minute-to-minute. You will not have enough hours in a day to get the things done that do need accomplishing...I can almost guarantee you that this will be the case. Or, you can take an hour each Monday morning (or whenever) and plan out your week. I think that you will find this one of the best spent hours of your week.

Plan things to do with your children. Some things can be spontaneous, but don't plan on relying on spontaneity forever. A good way to get some sound ideas is to try "brainstorming" with other parents that you know. It may even mean pooling your efforts and doing some things together. Some places give discounts for groups of a certain size. There are some good web pages with some great ideas, as well. Whatever you do...PLAN to do it!

Inertia will rule your life if you do not make plans. The words, "someday" and "sometime" only live in fairy tales. I have already noted all of the other things that are going to vie for most of your time each day. If you don't have any other plans, these things are going to conspire to consume your day. Only if you plan (and write it down) to go to the park with the kids from 4:00 to 5:00 pm. on Thursday, Oct. 23rd...ONLY IF YOU PLAN IT AND WRITE IT DOWN...will you actually do it. Sure, once in a "blue moon" you may "find the time" to take your children somewhere, but this is not how you want to bring up your children. God intends for this time that you have been blessed with to be used in raising your children in good, wholesome family time.

This brings me to my next point. Plan some time together; with the **WHOLE** (complete) **FAMILY**. This would include Mom, Dad, the children, and perhaps even Grandma and Grandpa. You don't have to spend money to have fun. There are many free parks available. These places are great for older and younger to interact. Museums can be free and can be a lot of fun if visited with the right attitude.

Even the things that do cost money can be shopped around. Use coupons and discounts. Ask for discounts. You will never know until you ask. The worst thing that can happen is that they may tell you there are no discounts today. Look for and take advantage of "open house" specials.

Go to something **REALLY SPECIAL**, from time-to-time, as a family. From this fond memories are made. Just don't get caught up in the entertainment trap. Little children get some of their biggest kicks out of a stick and a piece of string. They also may get a lot of fun from a free municipal park swing and slide set.

The point is (and this point must not be missed), use the time to do things **TOGETHER**. This will be some of the best spent and most wisely invested time of all. I do understand that, if you allow it, you have a lot of "important things" with which you can block in this whole twenty-four hour time period. Never, never, never consider that time spent with the children as "not so important"!

Family time can also (and should also) include time each evening spent addressing some spiritual matters. Some call this "devotions". Devotions can be different from family to family and often are. Devotions are not just a time where we read the Scriptures, (Although it does include this great idea). Devotions are times when a family can read a portion of the Bible and then discuss what it means and how it can apply to this particular family and even this particular child or adult. It can and should be a time when children can ask questions that have been on their mind, or discuss things that they have seen and heard at school, or on the playground, or in the home, etc.. Devotions can also include a time when parents impart their spiritual values to their children and a time when the children may want to point out a perceived inconsistency that they think that they see in one or even both parents. This is a great opportunity for the parents but the children should be trained to show proper respect for their parents.

Devotions do not happen naturally or automatically. Mom and Dad need to set a time to get together with the rest of the family. These times must the same for consistency. Everyone can politely remind others of the exciting time of devotions. In the long run, however, it's Dad's responsibility to follow up on devotions. If things have a habit of slipping his mind, Mom can certainly, respectfully, remind Dad of the time. It is frustrating for others to remind Dad and for nothing to come of it. Dads need to make Devotions high on his priority list!

Parents, do not be hasty in agreeing to do anything else by "Shooting from the hip." It may have been a good way to survive in the "old west", but it most certainly will end in disaster if you run your time management schedule that way. Think before you respond. Take the time to consult your schedule. Certainly there are emergency situations, but they should be few, and far between.

All of this is akin to buying a car. The salesman is pressuring you to buy **NOW**, but you know that you should spend some time in prayer, in discussion with your spouse, in rehearsing all of the pro's and con's. You must not give in to the pressure. If something is demanding a decision **NOW**, any decision could certainly turn out to be a disaster. Maybe it won't be a "disaster", but it probably would not be as good a decision as one that had been thought out and prayed about. (This coming from an ex car salesman).

This is the whole reason that we have a time management budget. We all should **CONTROL** what happens with our time (and money). Other people or other situations should not take that control away from you by pressuring you into a commitment that is not the best for the whole family.

A word of caution here: your word should be your bond. This is another very powerful reason why you want to see how it fits in your budget. You may produce conflicting commitments. You may be forced to drop something that had good reason to be in your schedule, because you have hastily promised someone something that is not as important, but your word is on the line.

I know a gentleman who will not make a hasty decision. He can be quite exasperating sometimes, especially when you want a quick decision, but there is one thing about this person. When he commits to doing something, it **WILL** be done. He doesn't bind himself to impossible or conflicting situations. Also, part of his philosophy is this, "If it is truly a **NEED**, I will do everything in my power to help. If it is simply an 'I want to', I may feel compelled to help and then again I may not". These are good rules to live by. There is nothing worse than over-committing oneself.

Make room for the Lord. It is God who has given you the original twenty-four hours. Why do we feel that we can greedily take His gift to us and run off in some corner and "pig out" on it without thinking of Him once in how we spend this truly valuable gift of time?

People spend hours upon hours watching useless programs on television; playing board games; reading trash; or watching brain numbing sports.

Both valuable money and time are spent in the pursuit of this thing called, "entertainment". Perhaps you totally disagree with me on all of the things that I have just mentioned, but answer me this: Do you spend half of the time and/or the money on things for our precious Lord and Savior, Jesus Christ?

It is the study of God's word which is going to prepare you and me for eternity (II Tim. 3:16-17). Just how much time do you spend in the Word of God, the Bible? I propose that people (in general) leave the study of the Word of God to "chance". Statements are made, such as: "I'll study the Bible when I get more time". Guess what? Many never get this valuable "time". It's bad enough that so many never study the Bible, but there are multitudes that never even **READ** the Bible.

In your schedule of time management, why not cut out a good sized piece of time for the **STUDY** of God's Word. Study will involve a Bible, concordance, maybe a lexicon, and perhaps an interlinear Bible, etc., etc...Study is more than simply READING. It certainly includes the reading of the Bible, but study tries to get the full meaning out of each passage. It isn't how many verses that you have read in any given length of time that really matters. The thing that means the most, is what you have understood and applied to your life (II Tim. 2:15). Let me risk boring you by stating this again. **YOU WILL NOT STUDY THE BIBLE ACCIDENTALLY.**

We certainly must include prayer in the list of spiritual things: the things that must be included in the restraints of time. The tangible, physical, empirical things of life have much more influence upon our decisions than the spiritual "pie-in-the-sky-by-and-by" things. So, if it's time to eat and get to work versus pray, eat, and get to work...what do you think will win the time battle?

The important thing to remember is this: That which **APPEARS** to be the most important (the physical) is actually the least important thing to consider in your prioritizing of things that need to be done. The most important things are the ones that our physical mind and eyes tell us are insignificant.

If you do not include a regular and daily talk with God in your schedule, your life will not be guided properly. The challenges of raising children will take on a new meaning. You will be raising these children **ALONE!** I really don't care if you are a husband and wife team, or not...you are both alone and on your own if you do not include God at the top of your priority list.

This prayer time needs to be quality as well as quantity. Little short, generalized phrases doth not a prayer make. Pray as though you were trapped in a well and the water was rising. Forget the King James language and the flowery speech. Also forget impressing someone else (if there is someone else in the room). Please do not be so silly as to try and explain the situation to God...**HE ALREADY KNOWS**...as a matter of fact, He knew before you did; He knows more than you do about the situation; He knows the solution or answer to the situation.

If you are praying with other people present (more than likely not, but it may be you and your spouse, anyway), do not take this opportunity to preach at someone that is present with you. Again, I say, pray as though you were in the bottom of a well and the water was rising!!! This thought would remove all of the foolish trappings that people have attached to the idea of prayer.

Lastly, on the subject of spiritual time management, leave room for quiet meditation. As with so many things of God, heathens have adopted things that are totally scriptural. Eastern religions have given meditation a bad name and Christians have shunned the concept because of this, but I want you to understand that meditation is, and always has been, totally Biblical (see: Psalm 19:14; Psalm 49:3; Psalm 119:97; Psalm 119:99).

What should we meditate on? Firstly, we should meditate on God; His goodness to us; His awesomeness; His creation; etc.. Secondly, we need to meditate on our life as it relates to God. Thirdly, we need to meditate on the Bible study which we have just finished: What do these teachings mean and how do they apply to…ME.

This kind of thing takes a goodly amount of our time…that is, if we do it properly.

Chapter 7
Standards and Convictions

We, as Christians, should have standards. Standards of godliness that have been developed from sound Biblical principles. Each one of us may differ, to some degree on those standards, but all-in-all, our standards should be somewhat similar. This will be especially true if we are taking our standards from the complete Word of God (as we should). When we read the scriptures and properly meditate on what we have read, we will then be able to apply these things to our lives. The bible can and will speak to us when we will give it a chance. The way the Bible "speaks to us" is in the read, meditated, and understood Word of God. (James 1:23-34). As we see this image of our selves we will see that we really need to start or stop doing some of these different things. This is called a "conviction" (conviction: a conclusion on a matter from the Bible that calls for action that we bind on ourselves…NOTICE…I DID NOT SAY "BIND ON OTHERS! The Bible can be and should be a living book for the twenty-first century, but it only can be if we can make Biblical applications of Biblical principles.

For an example, what do I do in regards to I Cor. 3:16-17: 16Know you not that you are the temple of God, and that the Spirit of God dwells in you? 17If any man defile the temple of God, him shall God destroy; for the temple of God is holy, which temple you are.

Again in I Cor. 6:15-20: 15Know you not that your bodies are the members of Christ? Shall I then take the members of Christ, and make them the members of a harlot? God forbid. 16What? Know you not that he which is joined to a harlot is one body? For two, said he, shall be one flesh. 17But he that is joined to the Lord is one spirit. 18Flee fornication. Every sin that a man does is without the body; but he that commits fornication sins against his own body. 19What? know you not that your body is the temple of the Holy Ghost which is in you, which you have of God, and you are not your own? 20For you are bought with a price: therefore glorify God in your body, and in your spirit, which are God's.

I personally apply these two passages of scripture to myself and conclude that I can do nothing that will harm, in any way, my physical body. Therefore, I do not smoke, drink, do illicit drugs, run out in February with no coat on, etc., etc.. You may not get that take on these two passages...THAT'S FINE! Rest assured that if the name "cigarettes" was in the Bible, satan would have just given the things that we know as, "cigarettes"...he would call them by another name so to thumb his nose at God.

I am not really writing a religious book, but these things do affect us and we need to apply them properly. All of this would take a good deal of study in God's Word, prayer, meditation, and of the Word which doesn't make excuses for our own desires. These standards are ours...they are very personal. If, however I believe them strongly enough and they are right as far as I understand, I should want to share what I found. Only share and **NEVER** try to compel another to come to all of my own convictions. Certainly I will want my children to gain some of these standards also. Applying a Biblical principle and coming to a conviction is not for little minds. There will come a day when our children will (hopefully) come to some good and strong convictions on their own. Until that day happens, we want to help hold to the standards that we want in our home. This chapter deals with these standards and convictions of the Pratt home.

You set the standards for **YOUR** home. "Devotions" are a good way to work in some of these Biblical principles. As I have already stated, little children may not understand **WHY**, but they need to understand and respect **WHAT** you and your mate's standards are. To some degree you can **TRY** to explain the why of your standards and your children may catch on to a certain amount of your explanation. As the children grow older, revisit the why of your standards. It will be necessary to revisit the "WHYS" several times. **DO NOT LOSE PATIENCE WITH YOUR CHILDREN!** There are different levels of maturity and understanding and different rates at which children attain to those levels.

When your child challenges your standards, rejoice...the child is thinking, this is good! Take all of the time you need to sit down and lead that child through a very deep study of The Word, and what your conclusions may be. A challenge (open or subtle) to your standards is an indicator that this child is ready to form his/her own personal convictions. They may not see things exactly the way you do, but make sure to study together and share your thoughts with him/her. **RESPECT** your child, even if/or when he/she disagrees with you. Have the child explain why he/she has formed the conclusion that they have. Help them keep the convictions that they do gain.

Keep the discussions kind, friendly, and very open. You want to create the desire in the child to come to you with questions and even challenges. They may even come up with some thoughts that you hadn't even considered before; thoughts which will help both you and the child to strengthen views.

Respect is always the order of the day. This goes in both ways. If your child has studied a subject out and has come to a conviction on the matter, be sure to respect that conviction…**EVEN IF YOU DON'T AGREE WITH IT!** One thing needs to be understood, as well, as long as any child lives under my roof, he/she **WILL** respect Mom and Dad's convictions and keep the standards that have been set for the family.

Any deviation from this rule will foster pure havoc with every other child in the family.

If your convictions and the convictions of your older child(ren) conflict, there will have to be a meeting of the minds. In general we would encourage the more conservative of the two convictions. We are speaking here of two completely different convictions on the same subject. We are **NOT** speaking of someone having a conviction and another party having **NO** conviction. Always the conviction should be respected over **NO** conviction. An example in which these disagreements might arise will be found in the areas of music and clothing.

You will find that your standards and convictions will come under attack and be challenged as time goes on. Just remember much of what you want will be challenged as children get into the teen years. Unless you have laid down and let the inmates run the asylum, you will get resistance. Do not bend your standards and convictions simply because your children whine in your ear. Put an end to the whining! In reality many times those children may not want you to bend, at all. Many times they are simply testing you to find out how deeply you believe this and how much you are willing to defend these standards and convictions.

If an older child leaves the home and rejects your standards and convictions, **DO NOT CHANGE TO ACCOMMODATE THIS CHILD! !** You are the beacon shining through the night. If he is ever going to find his way home again, spiritually, it won't be by moving the light house. Take a stand for what is right and do not change your standards, no matter the pressure that may beat upon you. This is one of the most horrible times that you could go through. Let us hope that you will not have to, but if you do... **DO NOT SNUFF OUT THE LIGHT.**

When you set your standards, be ready always to set the example. Children watch **VERY** closely. They do not take kindly to parents who preach one thing and then do another. Children are very idealistic (almost to a fault) and their little radar antennae are always out and receiving. Do not ever let situations affect your standards and /or convictions. If you make this mistake, you will have opened the "Pandora's box" of "situational ethics".

Be ready and willing to accept respectful (with the emphasis on the word "respectful" questions concerning your walk as a Christian. We adults are far too defensive. We DO make mistakes. It kind of hurts when those that we are trying to impress (our children) notice those mistakes. Admit when you have done wrong.

Nothing goes further to cement a relationship between parent and child than the truth that we all make mistakes. If we can admit ours, perhaps it will not be so hard for our children to admit and correct theirs. The Bible states: "Pride goeth before the fall!

Be aware that sometimes the child is simply testing your reactions. They want you to keep your cool, but they are also challenging your true inner spirituality. Don't react in the same mode as they do, or worse yet, don't best them in their own game of over reacting. Retaliation is not a "parent" kind of thing to do...it's a childish thing to do.

If your child can speak candidly with you from the earliest ages, he/she will continue the trend when they become teen agers. The teen years can be difficult, but if the lines of communication have been taught and practiced and left open, you will be able to deal effectively with your teen agers. Remember, in all this, YOU must "keep your cool".

Standards and rules also need to be set that are not spiritually oriented. Rules and standards can determine what chores get done and when; dinner rules, such as how we eat...when we eat...dining etiquette used as we eat, rules concerning visitors and permission to have visitors, etc.

Let us deal specifically with the idea of chores. It is your author's opinion that all children should have chores. These chores are not to be done for payment of any kind. The fact that all of the child's needs are provided by Mom and Dad should be payment enough. These chores should be done in a timely manner (that means that we don't have to "nag" at the child to do what he/she knows must be done. The job needs to be done well, not slap-dash. Absolutely NO arguing or back talk should be tolerated...NOT ONCE...NOT EVER! Any disrespect in any area needs to be soundly dealt with.

When you set standards and share convictions with your children, be sure to discuss the consequences of letting those standards down. We can deal with two aspects of consequences: Firstly, there are consequences in the home, from Dad and Mom to child. This may come in many different forms such as spankings, groundings, "creative discipline". Secondly, there are spiritual and eternal consequences for going against the standards and convictions which are based on God's Word.

When we discipline our children for violating those standards, we need to go over the reasons that we have for those standards. Again, we need to explain the consequences (both temporal and eternal) of crossing the line. The more that we can and the better the child understands, the easier will be our job in this particular area.

Standards in the home must be uniformly preached, taught, and enforced. Both parents must be "on the same page". This is why it is so very important for young, starry eyed couples to discuss the future in depth: their beliefs, their convictions, and the many other differences that they may have. They must discuss these things so that they will know how they will collectively handle problems in the future when they are trying to raise their family. These things need to be agreed upon, long before the marriage and long before the children come along. This is related to the process of agreeing on discipline.

Keep your standards standard. Don't change those standards and do not make exceptions for one of your children. Along with idealism, children have a definite idea of what is "fair". No child would be able to deal well with parents who show favoritism.

This is not to say that you, as parents, cannot make general blanket exceptions. Just make sure that these are **EXCEPTIONS** and do not let them become the "norm". Tor instance, your rule may be that no child can be out after 11:00P.M. (or whatever time you want to make as your rule. Maybe some important event is happening and the child will be with other adults that you trust. In that case you may want to make an exception. Make sure that if this happens to just one child and you have other children to whom you explain your reasons, you had also better be prepared to make the same type of exception with them. As they grow up they will remember the "exceptions" and those "exceptions" will become "precedents" later.

Be very careful as to what precedent you set. More than likely you are going to have to live with your decision(s). Exceptions (precedents) need to be only set in an extremely unique situation. It is possible to change precedent, but it will take a lot of work and good, sound, explanations as to just **WHY** this precedent goes by the wayside. The only reason to change or adjust a precedent is that the original setting of precedent has now brought some very unwanted (possibly sinful) results. You will need to show the other children what those results were and how they were sinful and/or dangerous. Spend time fielding questions and firming up your decision.

Once you have changed a precedent, your decision should be considered in the same light as any other standard or rule of the household. The new way of doing things should be explained clearly and any and all consequences for disobedience should be established. As with any other rule or standard, it is always best for you to have the children repeat back to you what they understand you to have said.

Correct any misunderstandings; deal with any bad attitudes; and then expect and enforce obedience.

The following paragraphs will include some rules, standards and convictions that we enforced in our own family. This is not done because I think that everyone should have the same rules, standards, and convictions that we subscribed to, but so that the readers of this book would understand where we were coming from. You may disagree with some or all of the rules; you may disagree with some and agree with others; you may even (most unlikely) agree with everything, but form your own standards and convictions and live with them.

Our children were not allowed to go anywhere without us knowing where they were going, who was going with them, who was driving, and what they intended to do when they got there, and just exactly when they intended to come back. Any change in plans had to be phoned in to us first, for approval. Any violation of these rules would result in grounding from any sorties in the near future.

We expected that if they were headed for the mall and that is where they told us that they were going, that is just exactly where their next stop had better be. If someone was thirsty and they wanted to go to a fast food place for a soda-pop, they needed to get permission from us as soon as possible.

NEVER were our children allowed to go "cruisin" up and down the "strip". I used an analogy of the cockroach who did not appreciate light and desired to be in some of the rottenest places. The cockroach came out at night when it was dark and scurried about doing his filthy work. Human cockroaches cruise the "strip": Drugs are dealt; drinking is all a part of it; sex is there; and illegal activities can be involved. If a great big floodlight, the size of the sun, was to shine on these human cockroaches, it is my belief that they would all scattered in about the same way as their namesakes. Our children were not going to be a part of this scene.

Later on, when our children did go somewhere specific, we required them to be back on later than 11:00 P.M...We did not mean 11:10, or 11:15 or 11:30. This rule had its reasons and we fully explained those reasons to our children. If one of our children came in late, we would listen to any reasons given for their lateness. These reasons had to be legitimate and preferably corroborated by someone else. Some people don't allow any excuses. I find that pretty unrealistic. I am sure that we all have been late...even as adults. If we, as adults, expect others to listen to our reasons, it should only be fair that we hear our children out. It is not possible to raise children with a rubber stamp. Be firm but be fair. Not giving any credence to our children...basically calling them liars, will only build up anger and resentment in your Children if you rule with an iron fist.

Chores were to be done each day. We made up a chart with the names of the chores lined up along the top. Down the side of the chart, we put the children's names. We tried to give each child a different job or jobs each day. If you make up a chart such as this, make sure that you try to be very fair and even handed with each child or you will be able to hear the Revolutionary War re-enacted.

Not only should the jobs be different, but they should be as evenly paired up as possible. There are some jobs which will be quickly and easily done. In your home there will be chores that will be harder or take a lot of time. There will also be jobs that have to be assigned which will be nasty and unpleasant. Garbage is a nasty job. Cleaning toilets is another nasty job. Some children see the washing of the family dog as a disgusting chore.

Cleaning the entire basement may be a very difficult job and might be saved for a Saturday "work day" for all of the family. These work days should include everyone including Mom and Dad. These "work" days can be set up to clean the attic; clean the basement; clean the grounds; tidying up the garage, etc., etc.. **NOBODY** should be allowed to leave until the entire job is either **COMPLETED** or everyone decides to stop (with Mom and Dad's approval.

Lying, cheating, stealing, or any form of dishonesty would not be tolerated. When our children were very little they would fall short in one of these areas from time-to-time and would need some correction. I can remember that one of our children hadn't quite figured out that if you say something in a store that you liked, you **COULD NOT** simply put it in your pocket. This child had a special fondness for grape gum. One day as we were either coming from or going to church, I smelled the very distinct smell of grape gum. After determining which child had the gum, I further determined that this child had shoplifted the gum. We marched the child back to the store, gave the unused portion back to the store manager and had the child pay the full price for the gum (without being allowed to keep the unused gum). I then asked the manager (privately) to give the child a good lecture on shoplifting, including the potential consequences.

All of this didn't work out, for it was not a long time after this that this same child shoplifted something else. This time I made the child sit on a bed in a room and told this child to imagine that this was jail. I explained to this child that this was similar to what could be expected if the stealing didn't stop. We did return the stolen item and I believe that the idea of being in "solitary confinement" got through. We had no more problems with this child, concerning theft.

We also encouraged our young people to go out together as a group of other young people. Young people should become friends and get to know one another in a group setting. Teen agers are being allowed to date one-on-one at ridiculously young ages. These are judgment calls on your part, parents. Don't be a dope! Along with this early age dating comes various degrees of unaccountability. We might expect this from parents that have no Christian standards, but Christian parents should be spiritually smarter than this. Don't allow your child to place him/her in a compromising situation, or for him/her to be placed in such a situation. Romans 13:14 says: Make no provision for the flesh to fulfill the lust thereof.

Later on, if one of my teens was going somewhere with someone of the opposite sex, we took great pains to know **EXACTLY** where they were going and they were **NOT TO STOP IN THE CAR ANYWHERE** while it was just the two of them and especially at night. **THERE IS ABSOLUTELY NO GOOD CHRISTIAN REASON FOR TWO CHRISTIAN YOUNG PEOPLE OF THE OPPOSITE SEX TO BE ALONE WITH EACH OTHER IN THE DARK, IN A STOPPED CAR!!!** As I say, however, that is just my conviction. You figure it out for yourselves. Remember...this is when you need to be a parent and not a **PAL**. I am not sharing all of this with you as a perfect parent...I am telling you as someone who has learned a very valuable lesson.

Put your foot down and do not let the teen ager in you life run over you!

With Dodi and myself it was hard because all of our daughters dated either after they had turned 18 or turned 18 while they were dating. When a child turns 18 the weight of enforcement shifts a bit. You can, however, still insist that they abide by your rules as long as they remain under your roof and eat your food and drive your car.

Something else that needs to be addressed is this: Really know everyone involved if you allow your child to stay overnight with someone. Consider the age of the child, the perceived moral qualities of the family you child is going to be staying with. I could say so much more, but this is not just a little ho-hum thing. **BE RESPONSIBLE!!**

You cannot always control the child's entire environment. The standards and rules that you are trying to instill in your child will be regularly violated. This can confuse the child. Have the neighborhood children play with your child in your environment, as much as possible. When the children do play in you home, make sure that you are ready to instruct these outside children in regards to the house rules. Make sure that you are also ready to send these little "darlings" home for infractions of these rules.

Again, I say: "control your child's environment as much as is realistically." Only in so doing can you set the standards and expect them to be adhered to. Allowing your child to be bombarded by different standards (or no standards at all) only serves to confuse your child and your child will challenge you and your standards if he/she sees that they are not universal.

Probably one of the most important standards that need to be in place is this: Mom and Dad are in charge. This doesn't mean that the children need to cower before you. I have seen this rule taken to the absurd. Remember this, you want to **EARN** your child's respect and love, not simply create a "slave/master" relationship. Children should be able to question things that the parents say, if that questioning is done in a respectful attitude. The important thing that the child needs to remember, however, is that once the final answer is given…**IT IS THE FINAL ANSWER**. Arguing with the parents is not permissible once the parent has said, "enough".

Parents are not the children's "buddies". You cannot properly teach your children or enforce your standards if you are going to try to be a child, yourself. Do not confuse your children by producing a relationship that should not exist. Later on in life, after your children are married and out of the home, you may be able to develop a very close friendship relationship. This relationship should be between two adults, however, not between an adult (parent) and a child.

There are so many other standards and convictions that we lived by, but these few should suffice as examples. Set your own standards. Make your own rules, but do not leave things to take their own course.

The standards that you set; the rules that you make; the convictions that you share with your children, will be in direct proportion to the adult that you produce from your efforts. Raising children is not a "cake walk", it takes input from you. If you believe that your standards and convictions are right, then you have a responsibility to instill these same standards and convictions in your children.

Chapter 8
Education

There is a raging debate today on the subject of education. Which school system is the best; what's wrong with this or that system? Better yet, what's good about this system or another? I do not select any one system over another system. Each system of education has its positive and negative aspects.

This I do say, however, no system will work properly without personal parental involvement! The converse is also true. Any system may work properly, for the child and for education, in general, if the parents are totally, personally, and completely involved and knowledgeable about what is being taught. This is especially true if the parents have control of the intangibles, such as moral values, judgements, and attitude formation.

It well may be that you, as the parent, will have to volunteer to help in the school just so that you will have your "ear to the track", so to speak. You may want to know just what kind of teacher(s) your child(ren) is/are being subjected to. It isn't easy for anybody (teachers included) to impart pure fact and leave out their personal slant. You need to know what that teacher's personal slant is and how It will flavor their teaching outlook. Perhaps they have an agenda that you will definitely want to know. Sometimes in this process you may make a decision to make some changes with the personal knowledge that you attain.

You may have to spend some time at home listening to the facts and thoughts that your child has learned. It may be necessary to respectfully correct any wrong values and thoughts on which your child has picked up. The important thing here is for you, as the parent, to listen very attentively and be sure that you are hearing the facts...not simply **WHAT YOU WANT TO HEAR!**

It is also important that you pick up on the atmosphere of the school, in general. Are there unsupervised opportunities for students to get into trouble (parking lot, bathrooms, gym {after hours}, neighboring businesses, etc..)? More importantly is this: Is your child threatened by, or participating in, some of these unsupervised activities?

As you well may have already guessed, I am, in general, addressing the public school system. One glaring problem that I have observed is this: Parents who attended public schools twenty or thirty years ago (or more), try to project the school atmosphere and the way the system worked in their "day". Things, in general, have changed and if you do not "get with the times", you may well possibly be subjecting your child(ren) to a real and present danger. Do not view **ANY EDUCATION SYSTEM** through "rose tinted glasses". Especially do not assume the best and ignore the danger signs. Graduates of secular teachers' colleges of today are being indoctrinated with some **VERY** liberal, secular philosophies. It is also possible that some teachers in a Christian school setting could have (unknowingly?) also been indoctrinated with some of these same ideas.

It is generally true that Christian schools do not seem to carry some of the same perils of the Public School system. However, may I caution you that this may not always be the case. Even though the Christian school will probably put forth a Christian ethic, there is always the possibility that individual teachers, knowingly or unknowingly, will bring to their teaching experience some of the flavor of the liberal teaching curriculum. Sad to say, in this day and age of exposure to all kinds of wicked fare found in the media, that some of your child's classmates may also add to an environment of liberalism. Again, the parents need to be **INVOLVED** and know their child(ren)'s whole environment in the system to which you are en trusting them.

Beware, also, that there are other dangers and threats that are not really connected with the teachers. There are just some dangers that can be present in some situations. When children want to wrong they will usually find the opportunities in which their desires can be satisfied. I have listened to a caller on a talk radio program disclose that he sent his son to a Christian school, only to have him get involved with drugs that were being sold by a deacon's son! This man's son is now doing time in a state penitentiary. Parenting throughout the school years does require constant vigilance. You cannot assume that the best will just naturally and normally happen.

Also, the word "Christian" carries with it many different nuances of interpretations. You still may want to sit down with your children and discuss the values that they are being taught. It may even be necessary to correct some doctrinal issues that have been presented to your children. **PLEASE** do not **ASSUME** that you and the teacher and the school are all on the very same spiritual "wave length"

In general, Christian schools may be better geared to teach the values that you, as a Christian, want your children to learn. On the other hand, however, you **MUST NOT PUT YOUR CHILD ON "AUTO PILOT"**, and assume that there will be no problems, whatsoever. This would be spiritually irresponsible of you, as a good parent.

Cost can be another important factor which will need a lot of consideration. A Christian must balance, on one hand **STEWARDSHIP** of money...

and on the other hand the charge to "raise up a child in the way he ought to go". Do remember that there are really three forms of education that is available to you. Also, even in the worst of settings you can insure that the right things are taught and absorbed. This can happen, but **BOTH PARENTS MUST BE INVOLVED** in reviewing what their children have learned. Yes, I know that this is a great sacrifice, but it is one that will give you rich rewards in the final analysis.

"Home Schooling" is the third alternative. Of course, the nature of the system is going to preclude some of the problems inherent in the other two system. The whole "home schooling" system is based on parental involvement. There are some problems with home schooling, as well.

Curriculum can be a challenge to the teaching parent. As with all of the other systems of education, you need to determine what values and doctrinal issues are going to be taught. Especially is this true if you are using materials to form your curriculum that are not especially spiritual. Even spiritually oriented companies may have material with in which you may not be in agreement.

These teachings may really go against your religious convictions. Possibly much of what you have been trying to instill in your children is in peril. You might even have to "re-teach" portions of some books that you want to use in your curriculum.

There are pre-packaged curriculum series. In these there isn't a lot that the teaching parent needs to do, other than testing and fitting the right level of curriculum to each individual student. The teacher will also supervise and test the child to make sure that the information has been understood to a proper and proficient level.

Other parents may choose to design their own curriculum. This takes a great deal of planning and thought. One needs to be very careful that the student is receiving a well rounded education from the materials you have chosen. I would advise the average parent to go with the prepared curriculum and only do a personally designed plan if that parent has some background in education.

If parents choose to go the home schooling route, they must know right from the outset, that at least one and preferably both parents are going to be deeply involved with the student's schooling. Moms are more often than not chosen to be the actual "teacher". Dads, however need to understand that they have a real role in the process Fathers should be there to inspect what is or has taken place. He should be a positive encourager to his wife who is doing the lion's share of the work. Dads can and should talk to their children to satisfy himself that each child has a good attitude, is applying himself to the school work that is before him, and is comprehending at each and every level of learning.

Those who may be new to home schooling also can have a multitude of questions and some real doubts about their decision to home school. A parent wants the best for their child and may feel that they have not chosen to go down the best road. My suggestion to new home schooling parents is for them to locate the nearest home schooling support group for encouragement and real help. The best place to inquire would be at the public library.

You may have heard of a home schooling family in your vicinity. It would be wise to pay these folks a visit and let them know what you are doing. Even if they are not part of a support group, they may be able to send you in the right direction

Also, experienced home schooling families could be of considerable help. Seek out the opinions and the advice of all the members of the family. How did it go for the parents and what problems did they encounter. How do the children like the the idea of home schooling. This would be especially good if those children have come out of another schooling system. They are more able to compare what they left with what they are doing at the present.

Home schooling will be a full time job. You will need to set a schedule that everyone can work within and really and truly spend the time allotted in actually schooling the children. Some states have laws that you should know and with which you will comply. Find out your rights as a parent in the home schooling of your children. There are legal organizations that help the home schooler for a very small fee. Ask other home schoolers if they have the address or phone number of one or more of these organizations.

In any case, your primary focus must be the proper, complete, and finest education that you can give them. To do any less is a travesty of the whole purpose of raising your children in a godly atmosphere. Home schooling is definitely not for everyone, especially is this true of those who are not fully committed to this plan.

The charge has been made that home schooled children do not interact socially. We have home schooled five children and all of them have graduated from high school and all are married and are making their way in the world, quite well.

During their growing up years, our children had many friends from the home school group and from Church and from the neighbor kids all around. At any given time there were usually at least one or two friends in our house. As a fact, our children were not just well adjusted with their peers, but also with adults. Our children, quite often would carry on intelligent conversations with different adults. If there was anything lacking in their social adjustment, you would be hard pressed to show me where.

As older teens they held down paying jobs and they got along well with their fellow workers. They were well respected by their peers and by their different employers, as well. All of the children were involved in community activities.

You do not need to go out of your way so that your children will have an opportunity to interact with other children of the same age. Involvement with home schooling groups, Church, and with neighbors around you will work well to round out their social interaction. Not only did our children have interaction with others, we made sure to control who they played with and what they were doing. A key to proper interaction is the ability to control the environment of that interaction.

A very good setting that we found to produce socially adept citizens was to get the children involved in a volunteer situation, either at a hospital, a library, a veterinarian, or some other business where people are being served. This provides interaction with many ages and genders and the learning of responsibility to authority other than parents. Young people seem to work better and practice their godly attitudes better when they are away from home.

Some have chosen some of the better known organizations that are geared to the young people, such as 4-H or Girl/Boy/Royal Scouts, etc.. Any kind of Bible study, youth group, service club group will help the child. Personally, we felt that age-peer groups were not as good as multi-aged groups. It was because of the peer pressure and influence that we had originally chosen to keep them out of the public school system to begin with. Peer pressure, which can lead to becoming the worst element in a group, can also be present in some youth organizations that are made up of only peers. If you really think of it, school years seem to be the only times in our lives when we deal almost exclusively with our own age group. Pre school years and all of our adult lives are spent working with and dealing with various age levels. Placing children **ONLY** in their own peer group is an artificial attempt at social engineering which has failed time-and-time again.

Now that we have taken a look at the three systems of education (albeit in limited scope), we should now look at some specifics that have not already been mentioned. I will not single out the particular system or systems to which these specifics may apply. If the information applies to the system of education that you have placed your children in, simply heed the advice.

Make sure that your child is being challenged to perform at his/her very best. Do not be afraid to push a child, just a little bit, he won't break. If your child's educational system does not challenge him/her enough, you can increase that scope with efforts from home. Nothing says that what a child learns in school is all that he is capable of learning. You can do this extra education in several ways. One of the best ways to your child is to involve him/her in hands on activities or jobs that require practical application of what he/she has learned in the formal school setting.

For example, you could give a child some real life situations which will apply the math that has been learned. Maybe you can work on halving a recipe for chocolate chip cookies. You could apply some geographic learning by having your child(ren) map out your next vacation or get-away.

You want them to figure out a route complete with mileage from point to point, estimated times of arrival, etc...You could have letters written to grandmother so as to utilize their writing, grammar, spelling, and punctuation skills. On and on the list can go, but it is important for a child to see that there is some practicality to this thing called school.

You can also speak with the child's teacher and suggest that they would challenge your child with some extra learning activities. You might very well have to push the teacher a bit, as well as the child. Make your child completely comprehend that their "full time job" is learning. Let us make sure that he is doing his job.

Make sure that both parents are completely comfortable and satisfied with whatever curriculum and educational system that your child is being exposed to. Seek out help if you are setting this curriculum for the first time. If the curriculum is being set by someone else, examine it. If a teacher of a school will not let you see the curriculum that is being taught (and always ready to go into depth on explaining all of the ins-and-outs), let this be a big red flag. Shout...scream...go to the top with your objections. If you are ignored or humored, **TAKE YOUR CHILD OUT OF WHATEVER SYSTEM HE/SE IS IN AND** If, however, the teacher and/or the school is receptive, politely (but unyieldingly) push for changes in the offensive curriculum. Seek out other parents and attempt to convince them of the need for change.

Parents need to enforce the completion of homework by their children. This **WILL** take involvement. It is my belief that a parent needs to check over the homework to see where the child is having difficulties. You, as the parent, **NEVER WANT TO CORRECT OR MAKE HINTS TO THE CHILD... THE CHILD MUST DO THE HOMEWORK.** Without this being done, the teacher could draw wrong conclusions as to where the student needs help.

If a child tells you that he/she has no homework and you find out differently, you must punish the child for lying. Whatever punishment that you have discussed is appropriate for the sin of lying and must be meted out. If the child states that he/she has done their homework in a study hall, ask to see the work. Punish any attitudes that are displayed towards you for checking up on them. You are the parent and your full time job is to see that things are done and done properly. There is to be no "sass" given to you for this.

If a child asks for help on the homework, do the best you can to help them understand a concept, **BUT DO NOT DO THEIR WORK FOR THEM!!!** The best way to help a child do homework is to bring them back to the beginning of the lesson that they are working on and find what concept, or concepts, the student has not understood. Explain the concept in as many ways as necessary for him to understand. Once the lesson is understood, turn the child back to the homework lesson.

If none of this works and the child cannot grasp the concept and cannot do the homework, set up a teacher-parent-parent conference to discuss the problem. Whatever happens, **DO NOT LET THIS UNLEARNED CONCEPT BE IGNORED.** Learning builds upon learning. If one concept is not learned, it will come back to "haunt" this child later.

Encourage your child to hold on to his/her standards in a hostile and unchristian environment. Always be in your child's corner in any conflict between school policy or teacher policy and the Christian standards that your child is attempting to display.

Jesus warns us through the Bible to beware of "leavening" action of unsavory characters around us. He doesn't do this just once, but repeatedly. How long does it take for those who claim to be Bible believers, to comprehend and follow the advice of the very Savior? We, as parents, need to know that this kind of things happens, and we need to strengthen our child(ren)'s position in a hostile world.

Be prepared to go up through the whole "chain of command", if necessary. Start with a teacher-parent conference. If there is no satisfaction to be had here, ask to see the principal. Even the principal is not the last appeal. Every public school system has a school board. Christian schools do have a board of directors. I cannot stress the importance of going in person and laying your objection(s) or problem(s) on the proverbial "Table".

In more serious cases, you may even have to seek the help of an attorney. Letters to editors and other newspaper articles can also put some pressure on the "powers that be", into giving in. Do not neglect the influence of your minister. Set up a time for you and him to meet with the highest school powers. It is also effective to involve other Christian parents that hold to the same standards that you do. Schools may be able o ignore one set of parents, but they will find it difficult to ignore a ground swell of objections from multiple sets of parents.

Be prepared to remove your child from whatever school system that will not respect Christian ethical standards. I know that this sounds drastic (and it is drastic), but you must not allow your child's standards to be challenged, belittled, put down, or compromised.

Some preventative medicine can be found in parent-teacher groups (by whatever name they go). Involve yourself in these groups and give input as allowed. Make yourself known to one-and-all, and be involved (in your own way) in influencing these teacher's decisions.

Your child is not in school to be "cannon fodder" or a "leavening agent" among his teachers and his peers. Most adults have a hard time in setting the proper Christian standards at work or in their recreational time. Think of this child in this way: Your child has been taught to respect and obey all adults and especially the "AUTHORITY FIGURES" IN HIS LIFE! Put yourself in your child's shoes. Mommy and

Daddy tell them one thing to do, and as soon as they get to understand this...along comes an authority figure telling them something different. **CHILDREN MUST HAVE THE COMPLETE INVOLVEMENT AND CARE OF THEIR PARENTS!** No ifs-ands-or buts!

Most often it isn't even the teachers that challenge you child to conform. It's usually his peer group. Children can be the cruelest to each other. The pressure on a child to "fit in" and be accepted by his/her peers is tremendous. You must be constantly aware of this pressure and counsel with you child(ren), (in some cases), on a daily basis. It is a great deal up to you to help your child keep his "self worth" in his own mind and to have you hold on to the standards that you want to see in him.

This pressure does not let up or go away. You may find that it will become unbearable for the child. Be ready to change his surroundings if need be. As home schooling may not be for everyone's child...so also...public schooling and even Christian schooling may not be for everyone's children. Do not let yourself become trapped in defending a system, simply because you child is in that system. Be alert and on guard for the danger signs.

YOU must protect this precious child from these kinds of pressures, as much as is possible. Be involved. You must know what your child is experiencing and be ready to step in, on behalf of your child. The natural course of events will not be in favor of a Christian young man or a Christian young lady, will **NOT** be to keep strong in the face of opposition. Parents must be there for their children at all times.

There are some whose reasoning would consider the welfare of a plant more important than the welfare of a young boy or girl (believe it). We protect young plants in a greenhouse environment, but we throw young children to the the proverbial **"WOLVES"**. Most of this is done so that a child can learn to **"SOCIALIZE"**. I have told you previously that children can learn to "socialize" without being immersed in every vile and wicked thing that the devil with the aid of mankind has invented. I beg of everyone...**PLEASE CONSIDER YOUR CHILD WITH AT LEAST AS MUCH RESPECT AND CONCERN AS YOU WOULD GIVE A PETUNIA!**

Let me take the time to address the idea of nursery school and kindergarten, If there is a parent at home (as there ought to be), all that these so-called schools can teach and much, much more can be taught in the home environment. Too often these "schools" are just another way to obtain free baby-sitting for the children of parents who (because of their overspending) wish to both work outside the home for more **MONEY**. I personally think that married couples need to commit to the sacrifice of raising children...BEFORE THEY HAVE CHILDREN. When they commit to the raising of children, they commit to not "farming" that child out to every "tom-Dick-and-Harry".

A child's development is guided by the parents. It the parents responsibility to see that every facet of that development is the very best for your child. One of the major parts of this development is the education of the child(ren). You, as a parent, need to see to it that everything is in place so that your child can excel as a well rounded and Godly young gentleman or young lady.

Chapter 9
Entertainment and How if Affects Our Children

There are some acceptable forms of entertainment and there are some forms of entertainment that are not only offensive, they are aggressive and just plain destructive to your child(ren). The biggest problem is that these differences are not being properly identified. .All to often parents are too busy to even notice with what their children are being entertained. The reason for this is that parents are not thinking properly and often are living back in an age when certain things were "all right", but times have changed and what was good, in the past, has taken on a decidedly evil connotation in today's world.

Some parents don't know the differences, themselves. They may not have ever been instructed on good and bad, from a spiritual reference. It is possible that we are seeing some poor judgments being handed down from one generation to another. Time to make adjustments!

Included with these parents who are ignorant, are the parents that just don't care. They like the wicked things that the world can dish up in the form of entertainment. If they are in love with this garbage, how in the world can we expect them to point out the differences that really are there? We can only work with the parent that cares and wants to be properly informed.

Criteria and standards need to be established and agreed upon by the parents, so that they have a chance to control what's being fed to their children. Of course, these standards will be subjective, to some degree. Because of this, many parents will make the mistake of not setting any standards at all, for fear of making a mistake. That is the easy (and might I say, the lazy) way out. Think really intently on this subject. If you take the easy way out, you **WILL** reap some real problems when the input from entertainment becomes output from the child!

Again, I do realize that the standards which we are addressing can be quite subjective. Let me share my views on this subject. There are many forms of entertainment and I will attempt to address some of them in this chapter, but understand that I won't be able to address all of these issues. Let me list the more obvious forms. There are recreational sports, plays and skits, movies, radio programs, board games, satellite radios, books, magazines, audio tapes, video tapes, cd's, DVD's, television, flying, hobbies, mall surfing, video games, and the list goes on, and on, and on, and…I believe that I have cataloged the more prevalent forms of the entertainment industry.

You will note many common good and bad points. This is because we are dealing with only one industry, entertainment, these things may seem redundant, but the point that I am raising is this: We parents need to open our eyes and not just see one side of any issue…especially is this true in these very critical times. It is my hope that you, as parents, will add to the list and look at the dangers of some of these forms of entertainment. Do not let the entertainment industry be a surrogate parent. Your child needs guidance from God through YOU.

Let's take some of this list and give some pros and cons with each one. Remember, there are pros and cons to almost everything. You need to weigh the pros against the cons and make a guiding decision in your child's life. It might even be good for you to sit down with your child and run down the pros and cons together.

Let us start with "recreational sports". The pros are: good exercise; socialization; teamwork; an area in which the child can excel; the excitement that is generated in playing the sport; and the chance to be a real role model for others that may be younger.

The cons (as I see it) are: danger of personal, bodily injury which may not really exact the price on each person until later on in his life; mismanagement of time; competition that can generate bad attitudes; money spent that the child really can't afford; and most importantly, while away from the direct oversight of the parents there is a chance that the child might do or say things that don't meet with the parent's (from God) standards of what is right and what is really wrong. "Situational ethics" come to the forefront and "bargaining with the standards" can destroy a number of standards that you and the child have lived by.

Plays and skits show up next in my list. The pros are: camaraderie (especially so if the child is involved in the skit or play); excitement; the ability to put one's self in another time and place and experience what that would be like; sometimes it may be a learning experience; it also is an entertainment experience.

The cons can be: fellow players may have less than acceptable moral standards; immoral actions portrayed by actors, such as: incest, divorce, theft, adultery, dishonesty, etc..; foul and offensive language; and the inappropriate use of time.

The pros to watching movies, videos, DVD's, and whatever Hollywood and New York City invents...the pros are: The ability to see things through someone else's eyes; excitement; could possibly be a learning experience; a means to escape the trials and problems of everyday life; camaraderie (especially can this be if done as a family kind of experience or if seen with good, moral, Christian friends.

The cons: Desensitizing a person's outlook on life, and desensitizing the mind to violence, sex, immoral behavior, etc..; the learning experience could be the wrong kind of learning experience; the camaraderie could reinforce wicked things among the wrong kind of friends; misuse of time: support of an industry which does not try to put forth the ideals and principles that we have; and last, but not least… **MONEY.**

Radio has been an entertainment medium for some time, and it still is. Radio has come, waned, and reinvented itself. Radio is a very real presence in young person's minds. The pros to radio, as I see them are: music lifts the spirits (even though it didn't quite get the job done with King Saul); it is informative; helps pass the time; and it is easily transported everywhere.

The cons are: very vile and sexually centered programming is available; Evil ideas are put forth which demand our attention; in some cases, it seems that we can't do anything else constructive at the same time; music and and does arouse our immoral desires; at the volume that some young people play their music, there is a real possibility of damage to the ears. All in all, we have a great misuse of brain power which could be much better spent. Would you or your child want to match, hour-for-hour doing good Christian deeds (visit the sick, feed the hungry, go to those who are in prison, etc..) for each hour of time that you spend listening to radio?

Who could find anything objectionable about a board game? I can find some things wrong with board games. As a matter of fact, the game I have even preached against, from the pulpit, comes under the heading of "board games". First the pros: great camaraderie; escape from everyday troubles and routines; sportsmanship; some games actually instruct; and there is, or course...the JOY OF WINNING! Now, here are some of the cons: Some games are "habit forming". I don't know if anyone has actually labeled them habit forming, but what I see in the players, gives me an idea that they are "hooked" on some of these games. The players seem to not be able to lay it down when large amounts of time have been spent and large amounts, yet, promise to be spent; very large amounts can and are often wasted; These times together pass as "fellowship" and over time could be the sole desire for "fellowship", crowding all other activities out; very bad attitudes can be displayed (such as a spirit of pride and arrogance).

I am going to spend one paragraph on the dangers and hazards to at least one board game. It's introduced to the unsuspecting as a **FUN** game. In this game, a board is used and a little "pointer" is used to spell out words. The problem is that we are told that we will be asking questions of the dead. The board actually will get out of hand and usually scare some people right out of their wits. Parents...I, as a parent, do not want my children speaking with the dead. It bothers me even more when the board takes on its own personality and signature. I've a much board game. It carries the name that should be applied to this game of Ouija....that other game is called, "sorry" and it is soooooooo much better.

Books can also be a good form of entertainment. In our present day and age, however, books seem to be replaced by all kinds of questionable forms of "entertainment". Very few young people will take the time to search out a good book and read it. The seemingly liberal and aggressive actions of the public libraries, across the nation, allow all kinds of objectionable literature, flying under the abused banner, "freedom of speech". It is peculiar to note that certain conservative literature is just not making it's way to the shelf. Now I do wonder just how this is happening. The pros of reading books are: excitement; learning; the ability to know what people of the past have thought and written; the ability to understand other times and cultures; and actually living the life of the characters. While some cons are: possibility of bad language; evil and immoral activities; inappropriate use of time; creating a fantasy world that does not match up with the real world; pride in knowledge; mind control by so of the less scrupulous types.

Magazines are all around us and young people **ARE VERY MUCH READING THEM!** The pros to some of these magazines are: they can be very informative; exciting; young people can identify with some that are in the magazines (sports figures, adventurers, etc..); and the contents of magazines become something that young people can have in common with their friends. I will now list some of the cons: possibility of bad language (language that you, as a parent have tried very hard to keep out of your children's vocabulary! ; various forms and degrees of nudity; immoral behaviors; foul and obscene language, (as the parent has defined as to what is foul or obscene); bad examples; inappropriate use of time; can even cause covetousness (especially when a catalog is in use); can lead to envy; and can be a total misuse of money.

Audio tapes and even **DVD's** are being replaced by other recording and playing tools. I could not possibly remain current in this field, but suffice it to be true that children have, are, and always will be in one form of player or another. Again the pros: can be fun to play and exciting; some machines can teach different things; can be good "common ground" for teen "fellowship".

The cons are: what you put in the machine is what you will get out of said machine. If we allow our children to load in garbage then we can expect our children to develop a taste for garbage; No matter what the is played and enjoyed, this still true: whatever music or talk you feed the player...that is what your children will be listening to. It's time, parent, to act like parents and not your childs best pal! Know what they are being fed; on a lower key, there is a problem with misuse of time; and misuse of money.

Video tapes also can be good or bad. The pros for video tapes are: great instructional tool; "Home movies" can be produced; can be fun to watch; able to store things in a moving picture format that will be lost forever without this medium; and can bring people together. Video tapes can also produce some bad things: entertainment videos can be as offensive (or even more so) as television or movies (there is all manner of sex, violence, bad attitudes, immorality, etc..). In some cases parents are bringing home x rated movies and when they least expect it, their little children are watching these same videos. Is it any wonder today that little three year olds can be as crass as a sailor? There is also the inappropriate use of time; inappropriate use of money (to rent); as with so many of these other entertainment mediums, it can embolden one to go further and further in a quest for "excitement". Let me say, at this point that the industry changes so fast that video's are already out. But rest unassured that the industry will produce something else to take its place (DVD's).

Television has become the entertainment of choice for the great majority of Americans. There is much good that the television can show, but, sad to say the media has become perverse in so many ways, it is hard to trust it.

Some who consider themselves Christians work hard to clean up the industry, others police it in their own homes, and still others just simply pull the plug. Let us take the time now to see some of the pros and cons of television programming. The pros are: excitement; the ability to put yourself in the action; learning; an easy way to pass the time; knowing and understanding what is going on in the world around us. The cons (as I see them) are: vile and wicked programming is available; it can be a tremendous waste of valuable time: the supplanting of our interaction with the family; it can be used to "baby-sit" and abrogate one's responsibility as a parent; learning of evil actions and attitudes; and a trend towards imitating what is seen in a program (It is my very firm belief that much of the violence that is displayed in society today has been learned on television) The industry leaders say, "not so"... they go on to claim that the activities on the T.V.

are a mere reflection on what is happening in real life (I ask you if you have seen more than one man murdered in one night? Indeed is this real life? Psychiatrists say just the opposite. Too much "copy-cat" crimes are occurring on an increased frequency. You make up your own mind on this issue, but it is serious!

Fun and frolic with friends was next on my list of entertaining things for our youth to do. Here we have camaraderie; fellowship; the learning of new things; excitement; and just a good way to pass the time. The cons are: some of the friendships are not with the best kind of people; some of the learning is what you (as the parent) don't especially want your child picking up; some of the excitement might be generated by things that are either illegal or immoral; and we have the ever present possibility of an inappropriate us of time and money. We won't mention drugs because a young person can get drugs in a group or without a group.

Mall surfing or just shopping, in general, is very popular with young people (and some older people, as well). The pros are: fellowship and camaraderie; the ability to purchase things deemed, "needed" (but I must advise you, if you didn't already know, that this is not the real reason to go "shopping"); fun and excitement; meeting other people; and just getting to know what's out there. The cons can be: meeting the "wrong" kind of people; getting into trouble; experimenting with immoral or illegal things; and there is always the possibility that your child...YES YOUR CHILD could be tempted to shoplift.

Travel is not always viewed as entertainment, but it can be. Its pros are: excitement; camaraderie (if done with parents and/or friends); it can be a real learning experience. The cons might be: travel with the wrong friends; and even though it could happen in your own back yard and in your own town, there is a slight increase in danger from attack by predators, getting lost, missing connections and leaving yourself open to all kinds of other major problems.

I put flying as a separate form of entertainment. I am speaking of flying in a private plane as opposed to public transportation. Many young people are getting their private pilot's license and some do it for fun and entertainment. The pros to flying are: excitement; learning; ability to see places that might not be possible without a license; and meeting new people. I do see some cons, however: danger; a possible really large inappropriate use of money and time; and a possibility of cutting off fellowship with other Christian youth who don't want to, or don't have the money to fly with you.

Hobbies are also a great form of entertainment. The pros to a hobby are: learning; being creative; fun; could even possibly make a little bit of money; and there is the opportunity for parents to interact with their children. I don't see many cons to hobbies, but there are some: The hobby could consume the person doing it; inappropriate use of money and time; and possibly a lack of socialization with other Christian youths.

When it comes to our child's exposure to all of the wrong things...even when the child is not setting out to be evil. Any and all of these things can be good or bad. The point;

PARENTS ARE TO HAVE THE

FIRST AND LAST WORD

CONCERNING WHAT IS FED

INTO THEIR CHILD'S MIND!

I cannot begin to reach the right pitch of **DANGER** that we are addressing. What you allow in your children you will get from your children. Know what you want and do not let anybody talk you out of it.

THIS IS YOUR DECISION

I should have prefaced all of my ranting with the fact that all of this stuff is your decision, not mine, not your relatives, not your good friends, and especially **NOT** anybody on a "talk show".

I have ended this list for the sake of space, time, and your boredom. The list can go on. This was only an attempt to get parents to try and see every angle that may be involved as a real and present danger for your children.

Men climbed Mt. Everest just because it was there. We, as parents, need to apply better reasoning in regards to acceptable entertainment. There is a lot out there and much of it is appealing. Probably the last thing that you need to consider, as a parent, is: "Is it appealing"? Your children will let you know if it is not. We need to know firmly and without equivocation...JUST WHY IS THIS ENTERTAINMENT THAT MY CHILD WANTS TO PARTAKE OF...ACCEPTABLE? IF YOU CANNOT ANSWER THIS QUESTION, YOU NEED TO REFRAIN FROM LETTING THAT CHILD PARTAKE IN THIS KIND OF ENTERTAINMENT UNTIL YOU CAN GIVE A GOOD REASON WHY IT IS ALL RIGHT

Make sure it is YOU that knows why or why not. You must not allow yourself to be manipulated by your child. Listen to their reasoning, but make sure that you do some clear reasoning before you make any decision.

One of the biggest considerations that should be made concerning entertainment is in the area of time. Time is precise, irreplaceable, and we will all be held accountable for our use of the time that has been given to us. Many things may be moral, legal, ethical, legitimate, fun, interesting, etc., etc.. These things may not justify the use of the time that would be necessary to participate. This is especially true if it takes our children away from Christian activities and duties. Our eternal judgment might very well hinge on what or how we use (or abuse) our time for God and others.

Stewardship is another big factor to be considered in the mix. No only is our time limited, but our other resources are also limited. Parents must ask themselves, "Is this the best use of my child's talents, opportunities, and funds". All things may be lawful, but there are some things that can be done that are more profitable than others.

This is such a subjective subject and decision that both parents must be involved to make it work. Young people, as a general rule, do not think clearly when making decisions that will affect themselves. Sometimes older people don't make good decisions either, but they are in a better position to make clear and wise decisions.

God has given children parents for many reasons. One of these reasons is that parents can draw on their life's past experiences and make decisions and judgments that are usually much wiser. This is not the case with young people because their age precludes past life experiences. Children chaff at this very reasoning, but nevertheless it is true.

Another thing that must be considered is (are) the surroundings. Where are our children going for their entertainment? I don't think that you would want your child going to a dance hall even if he was only going to play "ping pong" (I have been corrected by an oriental person..."table tennis"). Is your child traveling through "rough, bad, noted for evil, neighborhoods to get from point A to point B? Are the people who work in the establishments that your child prefers, the type of character(s) which you want as a influence in your child's life?

Might I take this opportunity to say, that if your intuition ("gut feeling") tells you that something is wrong, by all means, **GO WITH YOUR INTUITION**. I cannot remember a time that I went with my intuition and "kicked myself" later. I can, however remember the opposite. There is sometimes no apparently logical reason or explanation for this and your child will want to know **WHY**? Sometimes you don't even have an answer other than the fact that you just don't feel good about the situation.

This leads up to something else that your child is not going to appreciate. Go with your child the first time. See where he/she is going. Meet the people that are going to be around your child. Drive the route that your child is going to walk, bike, or later on…drive. Inform yourself, as much as you can, that you can make good decisions and be able to also rely on your intuition.

It is your responsibility, before God, as parents to raise up your child in the best possible conditions. This is going to take real involvement on your part. Do not assume, as your child might want you to, that just because "everybody else" is doing it, that whatever "IT" is will be totally acceptable when held up to your standards.

There are many things out there that catch the eye of a child and looks as though it would be worlds of fun and entertainment. Just because it is available; just because it's affordable; just because it IS fun; does not especially mean that you are going to want your child(ren) involved in "IT".

Most importantly, each area of our lives should be measured by it's value to our eternal destination. It is not one wit different with our children. We should be asking ourselves if what we are allowing our children to do will bring them closer to God or is there every good reason to believe that it may even draw them away from God…**FOREVER!** If there is a choice to be made, we need to be the parent that God has entrusted with **HIS** child. Looking at it in this light, we **MUST** make those decisions as God would make them.

As I said at the beginning of this chapter, the reason that this is such a problem for the children, is because some parents don't have enough (or certainly don't use) discretionary good sense. How can you expect a child to look critically at entertainment when his parents don't or even **WON'T**! Parents who spend the biggest bulk of their time doing what pleases them...their television shows; their videos or DVD's; their music; their games; and on-and-on! We not only need to look, with a critical eye at what our children are doing...we just might need to turn that same critical eye on ourselves.

Parents, make sure that you are setting the standard and living it. The example that you set speaks far louder than all of the words that you can say to your children. The entertainment industry is there to make money. It makes money. It makes this money by producing something that is greatly desired, interesting, exciting, lots of fun, etc., etc.. It is not guided by any standards or morality. These industries only rate things because we have insisted on it. You, as the parent are to be that guide. Make sure that you are doing your God given responsibility.

All fun is not sin...BUT...all sin carries with it a sense of pleasure (fun?).

The entertainment industry, in general, does not care about the damage and evil effects it will unleash on our children! There are so many alternatives out there that are, for the most part, overlooked. Might I leave you with some suggestions of things that still can be done by both parent and child? These things can replace or act as entertainment in your lives.

You and your children could: go on walks together; go hiking; canoing; bird watching; camping; fishing; hunting; teach the names of the trees, birds, and plants to your child (this, along with the ability to distinguish between each one and some benefits of each one); watch stars, meteorite showers, eclipses; learn the different phases of the moon; chart the movement of the sun in one year's time; play ball (any kind of ball); learn how to play a musical instrument along with your child...take lessons together and practice together; buy good musical CD's that meet godly and personal criteria...listen to them together; sing songs together as a family (maybe even learn different parts); make sure that the majority of evenings and days are spent in some kind of activities that have godly value; steer you child (and yourself) away from self-centered, "loner" type activities. Do things together that will uplift and encourage one another; have Bible devotions (try to find one of these "daily devotions" booklets and expound on them) "Our Daily Bread" maybe, for starters; Sing together, as a family, Who knows, you might become a "Trapp Family Singers" type group; do something nice to someone(s) as a family and as a big surprise; do some general chores together (clean out the garage, rake the lawn, make snow sculptures, etc.. Own and have everyone care for an animal (yes, I said **EVERYONE**); read good books together; take reading to the rest of the family (take turns at this); do crafts together (hobbies could fall into this same category). In short, do the very things that you and your children like to watch others doing on T.V.. Live life...**IN CHRIST, AND AS A FAMILY!**

Chapter 10
Friends, Socialization, and Dating

If all of your children are still very little, you can sleep through "Dating 101". There will be information, however, before we actually get to the dating part of this chapter. You might do well to read these and apply some of them, not only to the "teens", but also some of the wee ones.

Know your children's friends. By this I do not mean that you should only try to know what their names are. You should know what their disposition is. Observe your own children at play with their friends. Is this friend "bossy", irritable, rude, etc.. When the children get older, this is harder to do, but try to "weed out" the friends that constantly display undesirable characteristics. Certainly we want to give these children a chance first, to redeem themselves, but if that doesn't work out...help your children change their "friends". Teach them (as best you can) how to choose their friends. This is a skill that some adults have not yet mastered.

Firstly, find out if these friends have any kind of religious background (assuming that their involvement with spiritual things is important to you...if not...skip this step). No matter what their family life is like, encourage good spiritual things, as much as possible. Perhaps: prayer before meals, playing "Church"; having the children share their beliefs with you present (to guard hurt feelings on everyone's part).

Expect godly behavior while they are in your home (and when your children are playing in their homes). Vile, evil, hurtful, and unchristian attitudes and words and deeds, should be grounds for the offender to be sent home. Please, however, try to help the situation out for a time. Only if the other child will not cooperate would you entertain the thought of sending him home. They should only be allowed back upon them agreeing to the rules. You also need to have a talk with their parents so that everyone knows what's expected. If the parents won't cooperate, then it is probably better to gently break off relations with their little friend. I know it's hard on everyone, but it's easier to do it first off than to wait and excuse it for a long period of time.

Continuing the thought, whether there is problems or not, get to know their parents and what they expect. Again, you will make your teens blanch at this "old fashioned and very invasive idea". It is still necessary to get to know the other child's parents. So often the child is a (do we even know what this stuff is...) "carbon copy" of the parents. It will better prepare you in understanding and dealing with the child when that child is at your house. If the other parent has some rules for their children, respect those rules at your house (providing they don't offend God, in some way).

Next, try to figure out who is influencing whom in this relationship. If the friend is influencing your child, be very careful as to what is being taught in this relationship. If your child is influencing his/her friend, make sure that your child is passing on right, proper, and Godly values. Be ready to step in with some instruction if you find that necessary. Especially is this true when the children are very little. So often our children cannot explain what or why they know is right. They do not know just why we do or don't do some things and do or don't do even some other activities with which, the friend is not familiar.

As parents, we need to be very careful that the activities in which our child is enrolled, generally, reflect the values, morals, and tastes that are a part of your and your child's life. Do your "homework" before you place your child in a situation which might naturally lean away from what you want him to adopt as normal and good standards. Many a child has been damaged sexually and/or emotionally, because the parents trusted another adult and allowed that adult to usurp the parental authority and responsibility. Parents want to assume the best of everyone. For this reason they may be remiss in starting "trouble" with the youth group leader and/or the coach. Your child is far more important than the disruption of the child's youth group leader; the coach; or anyone else, for that matter! I would take any kind of offense on the part of the person placed in authority, as certainly a "red flag".

Assumptions, in general, are almost **ALWAYS VERY BAD**. A person wants to base any decisions or plans on solid evidence. Assumptions leave some of the basic groundwork of a decision, to chance. We need to be there for our children's sake. We need to look, listen, see, feel, and understand in just what our children are immersed. Many times the activity may be fine; it may be fine just the rotten attitudes that are not so fine. You won't know this unless you become involved, to some degree. Make sure that you are not using these activities as a "baby sitter", however. If you disagree with me on this issue, please reread chapter one of this book to know why I say what I say.

This is also where listening...true listening which involves listening to everything (silly talk, irrelevant issues, etc..). This kind of "listening" also involves asking questions. We need to ask questions about what was said and/or done. In short, we parents need to stay on top of everything. Our children do not live in a vacuum and we should not, either!

Doing the "right thing" may not always feel good. You may feel overprotective, or like some kind of "rat" and/or a "troublemaker". Do understand that self image may be a part of what you will sacrifice in the proper upbringing of your children. Know this; however, there is nobody else out there who will look out for the **TOTAL** well being of your children. Remember, these are young sprouts and saplings. They cannot be put out into a hailstorm, yet. They **MUST** be protected and nourished, still.

You wouldn't be a human if you did not wonder and doubt yourself. I am reminding you that you are charged, by God, with this responsibility. If your children grow up with wrong values and with the wrong type of friend, part of the responsibility rests with us for our lack of being totally involved.

So many men and women in prison are there because their parents did not take their responsibilities seriously. There are consequences to your actions...both good and bad consequences. What you do when the child is still young will form so much of that child's adult standards. Can we afford to feel self conscious or timid when it comes to making sure that our children are associating with those who will be the very best influence that child could have?

The home is still the best place for children to get to know one another. By this I do ot mean for the parents to run everybody outdoors where they cannot see or hear what is going on. If your input and supervision doesn't matter, why not send them off to a day care center (I am being facetious, here).

In business, they say that there are three important factors to consider whenever one is going to start a business. These three factors are: location, location, and location, there are three important factors in the socialization of your children. These three factors are: supervision, supervision, and last but not least...SUPERVISION! If children would do everything properly on their own, there would be no need for God to provide a child with **T W O P A R E N T S** ! Outside of the home atmosphere, you cannot be assured of what is going on, with whom it is going on, how long will be going on, etc., etc.. Outside of the home atmosphere, you really have lost control of the situation and have placed the responsibility into someone else's hands.

If you do things at home with your children and their friends, you should try to make plans for activities. Spontaneity works only for so long and then little Sammy will break his toy wagon over Bobby's head. When you plan fun things for your child's friend you control the input. You can teach spiritual lessons and teach value judgments that you want your child to learn. It will be challenging to come up with fun, interesting, exciting, and value packed things to do each time the children are together but there are helps available to you.

Most Christian book stores have activity type books (usually intended for the "Sunday school class"). Make your activities a type of class for the children. You say...,"WOW" , I'LL NEVER HAVE THE TIME TO DO ALL OF THAT"! You will if you take the other portions of this book seriously. I refer to chapter six (Time Management); chapter one (Raising Children Is An Unselfish Task); chapter two (The Home Front {What A Child Learns At Home}).

It can be done. It can only be done by a dedicated; self-sacrificing; well managed; individual. No, maybe you can't do it if you continue to do everything the way that you have always operated. We must set our priorities, BE WILLING TO SACRIFICE ! Stop moaning about the impossibility of everything that may be a little difficult. We limit ourselves so much when we make self-fulfilling prophecies ("I can't, It will never happen, etc...).

After reading what I just wrote, my wife says, "I think that you should encourage more spontaneity". Let their imaginations run without adult input. Spontaneity will find the children putting together a play or building a teepee, or producing their own "radio program" (on a tape recorder), or playing

("Church"). She is of the opinion that she only had to watch (inconspicuously) for bad behavior. What does she know; she only raised and home schooled five children from K-12, and at present heads up a Christian school? Should I listen to her?

Sometimes this will work. It will have a better chance of working as the children get out of their "toddler" stage. In some situations and with some children, I still am convinced that it will not work all that well. In those instances, I do believe that the parents will have to have some input in the situation. Pertaining to things in this area of raising children, you (as parents) are going to make the decision of which way you are going to deal with the overall situation.

If the children are using their imaginations and are behaving in a good and proper way, do as my wife suggests...simply observe from a distance. It is truly possible for a parent to "choke off" an active mind with a lot of pre-planned activities. Each situation is somewhat different, but the principles of proper child rearing still apply in every situation.

As the children grow older, it is very important to know **WHERE** your child is at all times. The time worn question goes somewhat like this: "where are you going; with whom are you going; what will you do when you get there; when will you be back at home"? Every item of this question **MUST** be answered. To your satisfaction...not to your child's irritation. It is not for you to be concerned that your child is irritated. It is for your child's safety and well being that you ask the questions. With age will come understanding and maturity and that will satisfy all, then.

Rights to privacy come when one has grown up and left the security and care of the home. Your responsibility, as parents, is to do your job. You must not be intimidated by older teens. Older teens have dipped into the waters of adulthood and now they want **EVERYTHING**. There is very good reason why society, down through the years has made "age of majority" from eighteen to twenty one. We are not defending one against the other, we are simply stating that parents are responsible for any children under that age. In later years, the child becomes an adult and goes from home and makes his/her way in life. As much as you may be so tired of "fighting" your children, the law still holds you accountable and so does the Lord, God.

With that responsibility comes authority. You cannot supervise what you cannot scrutinize. Do not hesitate to check up on your children. Check up on your child when he/she has gone out. The less infractions of the rules, the less you have to check up on your child. **NEVER** start to believe or say, **"MY CHILD COULD DO NO WRONG"**! Any child placed in the right set of circumstances **CAN, AND WILL DO WRONG.**

Any changes in the itinerary need to be approved. Give you child some change to enable him to make a call home. In this day and age, cell phones take away **ALL** excuses.

Your child needs your permission **EVERY TIME HE DEVIATES FROM HIS REPORTED ROUTE! !** Hold him to it. Any violation, no matter how big or small...**IS TO BE CONSIDERED A SERIOUS VIOLATION.** All violations should carry some form of fitting punishment. You must be fair to the child. Sit down with him/her before the situation arises and go over the punishment with your child. Make sure that they know, beyond any whining or tantrums, which you are going to apply the understood form of discipline.

There should also be punishment for bad attitude and an especially **BAD** punishment for sass. If this is the first time that you hold them to this, you **WILL** have a hard time. What you raise from the age of four is what you'll get at the age of fourteen. Please don't make things worse by giving in to the teen ager!

I know that you will feel sneaky if you check up on your child, but you must do it anyway, **FOR THEIR SAKES.** You don't have to make yourself obvious, but that son or daughter of yours had better be where he/she said they were going to be. Also note with who your child is. Make sure that there are no additions or subtractions from the planned roster of attendants, without you knowledge.

Now we come to the "dating game". You and I are going to have some disagreements. You are in charge. Be careful, however, that you are insisting on your way because you are scared to do it the "right" way. At this moment, I wish to very highly recommend the book, "I Kissed Dating Good-bye" by Josh Harris. Let me say this to all of you parents who dated and married by the world's standards: Do you want your son or daughter to do all that was "normal" in your day or in this day?

If you want your children to do what is right in the sight of God, perhaps you should **NOT** be holding up that which you have done as a standard. Either you want your child to walk in your footsteps (including all of the sinful errors that were associated with this thing called, "dating"), or you want to help your children blaze new ground in a Godly and pure relationship. If that be the case, forget your past and try to follow some of the advice of Mr. Harris and some of the thoughts that I wish to share with you in the remainder of this chapter.

My wife and I have four daughters who have all married four good men. These men are all leaders in the Lord, some are preachers. We had three different situations leading up to marriage.

Even though you have done your job and raised your children with the standards that you want to see, this does not ensure that those same standards and rules are going to also be had by that young man or young women your children will "fall in love" with. This can pose a real problem. The best that you can hope for now, is that this person will respect you enough to respect your rules and that your child will "come through the test". If your child is over the age of majority in your state, you will want to hope and pray that what you have taught them will prove the test.

Parents, do your best to stand by your standards and possibly avoid a tragedy. The very best of spiritual people can become carried away in a moment of passion. All of you know what is good and pure and holy; set your standards by what you know, and not especially what is popular at the moment. Look for encouragement from others whom you know and trust and who have good, strong standards, themselves. Make sure that you also are an encouragement to others who are going through this same situation.

I encourage group activities that will lead up to a one-on-one relationship. Friends going bowling or sledding, or singing at a nursing home or even out in the mall just having a good time is what I would encourage. These teens need to laugh together, cry together, and just get silly together. They need to hear each other expound on different subjects. They need to talk about convictions and everything else pertaining to life and death.

One of my rules that my children were expected to utilize, was that they needed to note that "special" person express himself/herself in good times and in bad. Specifically, I told them to observe this person when he/she got mad...got tired...under stress. This can be done in a group setting without anyone designating another person as their, "property", first. Young people should be friends...AND NOTHING BUT FRIENDS...first.

So often the problem is not with the young people, but with the older people playing "matchmaker". Adults, and even adults in the Church, have cause tremendous problems, a lifetime of problems, by not allowing young people to just be friends, first. Cupid still lives on in the hearts of older people who try to live other's lives in a sort of vicarious manner. LEAVE THEM ALONE, "CUPID"!!!!

I think that it's wise to start at an early age, fostering the idea that it is all right to NOT have a "girlfriend" or "boyfriend". If that attitude is encouraged, why would one be surprised when the child gets a little older, that he/she will "die if I don't find somebody"? I'm sorry, but I think parents who foster this kind of attitude in little children because they think that its "cute" are STUPID!!!! What this attitude does is drive the child to desperation when desperation is not really the case, at all. They become so desperate that they make some very poor choices. These kind of parents are opening a "Pandora's Box" that would have better have been left closed. Don't worry, unless your child is some kind of weird freak, they will find the drive, at some point in time, to search out someone of the opposite sex. You don't really need to help this along, at all.

If a young person expresses an interest in someone of the opposite sex, encourage your child to keep it on a friendship basis for as long as is possible. If they don't let on (or you don't let on), they will get a better and more honest response when observing that person.

INTIMACY AND SEX IS FOR MARRIAGE...AND ONLY FOR MARRIAGE!!

Cars are a form of transportation. They are not intimacy booths. They are not intended to be the room where secrets are shared. If you have two people in a car with no light on and nobody around (outside the car), You have a spiritually ticking time bomb!!

This "time bomb" is just waiting to go off. It does not matter how good and spiritual a person may be, when hormones are set loose in a young person, sex happens. Flesh is at war with the spirit. If two people of opposite sex place them in the perfect environment for sin...they will sin. Why can't parents remember back to their youth? Yes, this was somewhat different then...BUT NOT ALL THAT DIFFERENT! Romans 12:17b says "Provide things honest in the sight of all men". Romans 13:14 goes on to say, "But put ye on the Lord Jesus Christ, and make not provision for the flesh, to fulfill the lusts thereof".

If you call yourself a Christian and you say that you want your children to act as Christians should act...HOW CAN YOU ALLOW (AND HOW COULD YOUR CHILD DESIRE) TWO PEOPLE, OF OPPOSITE SEX TO SPEND LONG PERIODS OF TIME ALONE IN THE BACK OF A DARK CAR? ?!!!

Perhaps I'm being to harsh. Perhaps you and your child do not understand this. Let me explain: Darkness is the perfect incubation medium for evil. **PARENTS NEED TO TURN THE LIGHTS ON!** Make sure that couples always stay in the light. There is absolutely **NO** valid reason for two people of the opposite sex to be in the dark, alone, together. This is true, no matter the setting: a car, a room, whatever other place they might find.

All Christians should be accountable. This is especially true of young people who are interested in each other. The new name for this is: "to clarify" or to allow people to see into your relationship and not be with shame. There still is no reason for two people to go, on their own, together. If they need privacy, have a friend on the other side of the restaurant while this couple talks. It **CAN** be done, but so many do not want to "clarify".

I have heard young people protest that they don't have any intentions of doing anything wrong. I certainly can believe them. There are two problems with this idea, however: 1. The best intentions can and have (many times) gone right down the tubes when the hormones call. I mean it! I have seen exemplary, Christian young people...people you would **NEVER** think would be able to get in trouble...I have seen them destroyed!!! 2. Our lives are a witness to the rest of the unsaved world. It isn't always what you are doing; it sometimes comes down to what your neighbors **THINK THAT YOU ARE DOING!**

<u>**Remember Romans 12:17, "Provide things honest "in the sight of ALL MEN".**</u>

What a shame it is for some parents to let down their guard just a few steps from victory. You have raised your child, protected your child, nurtured your child, and guided your child through all of these years. Just remember: The future is not the present until it happens. Your child is not yet married until they say their vows. They are not married just because they have agreed to "live together". What you have worked so hard for is going to shortly culminate in a beautiful wedding. Don't you or your child throw everything overboard when it's this close! If you don't or won't step in and try to head the situation in the right direction, who will?

Bless your soul. I know that you want good, solid, information from other parents. The problem, many times, is that those very references have thrown over the cart. You have to rely on God's teachings and on the character that you have acquired over these many years. This is where it counts the most.

We sometimes can talk ourselves into a belief that we have done such a rotten thing in the raising of our children. We see everybody else as "having it all together" and we are "messing up". This is not the case. If you are even concerned about this, you haven't "messed up". Determine what is to be done, independently of what others may do.

These all may well be taking their queues from the world. In essence, then, by following them so closely, you would really be following the world. What has the world ever done in a good, godly way, with no regrets?

Nobody said any of this would be easy. Some things that a parent has to do are the hardest things that they will ever be called upon to face": spanking that cute little cherub, saying no when you know it will break their hearts for a time, holding you child to the right standards...even when that child already feels that they are an adult and should be given the "rights of passing" into that state.

    Never mind what that child thinks or says now. I've been there. Believe me things will get better as time goes by. Stand by what you know to be right. Don't back down and do not soften the rules because you think that they are too harsh and too "confining". Be strong and of good courage. Face your child and let him know that you will enforce all of the rules, **BECAUSE YOU DO LOVE HIM OR HER!**

Chapter 11
Submission

This probably should have been the first chapter of this book because it is so basic and ever so important. Submission is something that adults have a real problem with, and I believe it is because, as a child...they never were really taught to submit to authority. This is really sad because submission is really an important part of life. In some cases, we can find ourselves in a "heap of trouble" if we refuse to submit.

We not only need to submit to our parents, but we also have bosses that demand it. You cannot expect to argue with your boss on every little thing that you are told and then expect to continue to work at your present place of employment. Not only is this true of the "big boss" or the owner, but it is also true for the foreman, leadsmen, supervisors, etc.. There are even some that we don't have to submit to, but they can make your life **VERY** interesting if you don't at least have them think that you are submitting to them. The "girls" in the office can make for very interesting paycheck mistakes. The work place is replete with authority figures and we need to learn, long before we get a job, as an adult, to submit to these authority figures.

If one joins the military, on will learn quite quickly that one has to submit to those of a higher rank. If one does not submit in the military, one can be disciplined with all kinds of things and even a "Court Marshall". One can be Court Marshaled for what is known as "insubordination" which means forgetting the pecking order. It is **NOT** a light thing for one in the military to have an unsubmissive attitude.

We must submit to the laws of the land: local, state, and federal. Police officers demand submission to their authority. For those who will not submit to the authority of the law, there is another authority with which they **WILL** have to deal...the authority of the prison officials.

All too often, I, in my prison ministry, have to try and work with inmates who may still not get it. It all comes from the situations in which the parents have allowed their children to "sass" (talk back) and rebel at the parent's authority. These young men did not learn this kind of attitude over night. It took many years for a parent to train their child to be this rebellious. It comes as a result of not teaching the child that he/she must submit to authority. In the end, this child will probably break their parent's hearts. The same young adult will be one of the ones to populate the prison system. They will be submissive in the end, but only because of the force of the system that will be brought to bear by the penal system. The final babysitter!

When a child is not taught to submit to authority, they learn that they do not have to respect ANY authority! It begins in the home with the child disrespecting the parents, but it may end in places that we don't even want to think or, as parents.

Unsubmissiveness breeds intolerance for any and all authority. You cannot have a child learn that he/she needs to obey all of the other authority figures in his/her life, but they can disrespect you.

There will be many bad bumps on the road of life for the child that does not learn to be submissive. These young people will grow up and butt heads in all manner of relationships. It won't be simply a problem between parent and child.

God's word tells us that we must submit to the authority of the leader(s). We see so many problems that are created in the Church when it has rebels who will not follow the authority of God's appointed leaders.

Churches regularly split over the question of whether the people will follow the leadership of the Church or do their own will. Just a larger example of unsubmissiveness, usually.

In the family, we see that the husband is to submit to the will of Christ. This is not just a passing remark of the Bible, by a male chauvinist pig named Paul. Christians would argue this point to their ultimate peril. This dictates that the husband must be in **VERY CLOSE CONTACT WITH CHRIST**. This can only come through prayer. This is the only way one can be in close contact with the will of God. If he is going to be the spiritual leader of the family, as God would have him to be, he needs to spend a lot of quality time filling his mind and heart with the things of God.

The wife needs to learn to submit to her husband. This can be a very hard thing for a woman to do. Especially is this the case when the husband does not or will not fulfill his end of the relationship. The wife still needs to do what God wants. If little girls are not taught to submit to their parents, teachers, and religious authorities, what makes us think that they will submit to their husbands, later on in life?

Submissiveness is a learned response that comes from a humble and God fearing person. Submissiveness is for children, women, and men. Even when Christ was on earth, we are told that He was submissive to the heavenly Father. Children need to be taught to obey all authority figures; Wives also need to learn to humbly submit to their husbands. Men need to submit to God's leading. Even Jesus

Christ showed his submissiveness to the Father, when He prayed for Himself and His followers (in the garden).

Children need to be taught to obey authority figures. If children are ever allowed to sass or talk back to their parents or their teachers, they will talk back to the police, the preacher, or their husbands later on in life. Raising children properly, demands that the parents teach and practice submission.

Notice that I said teaches and **PRACTICE**. It is as with everything else; if you say one thing and do another, children are not going to follow as much your words, as they are going to follow your example. A man who is always grumbling about his work, or his boss, is not submitting to authority. A wife who treats her husband with disrespect and disobedience is not teaching submission to her children. After all, why should we expect our children to behave any differently than we do?

The children should see mom looking to dad for instruction and leadership. She needs to try to follow the wishes of her husband. Never should she be openly critical of her husband, and especially, **NEVER BEFORE THE CHILDREN**. Even if he makes what she considers, "hair brained" decisions, her responsibility is to see that his decisions are carried out. Any discussion should be with him and her only and in total privacy.

He, on the other hand, needs to submit to her emotional needs. After all, is this not what love is really all about? The husband is to love his wife as Christ loved the Church (The Bible says in Ephesians 5:21-28 KJV: 21. Submitting yourselves one to another in the fear of God. 22. Wives, submit yourselves unto your own husbands, as unto the Lord. 23. For the husband is the head of the wife, even as Christ is the head of the church: and he is the savior of the body. 24. Therefore as the church is subject unto Christ, so let the wives be to their own husbands in every thing. 25. Husbands, love your wives, even as Christ also loved the church, and gave himself for it; 26. That he might sanctify and cleanse it with the washing of water by the word, 27. That he might present it to himself a glorious church, not having spot, or wrinkle, or any such thing; but that it should be holy and without blemish. 28. So ought men to love their wives as their own bodies. He that loveth his wife loveth himself. 30. For we are members of his body, of his flesh, and of his bones. 31. For this cause shall a man leave his father and mother, and shall be joined unto his wife, and they two shall be one flesh.

The wife still needs to do what God had in mind, even when the husband doesn't keep his end of the command in Ephesians. The wife does what Christ wants, not because her husband may deserve it, but in love to Christ and following His plan both for her and for the children. Let me say to you at this time that things in this mortal life are not always fair. Do not confuse the rewards of this life with the eternal rewards of the next.

If little girls are not taught to submit to their parents, teachers, and spiritual authorities, what makes us think that they will submit to their husbands? I can feel the broken hearts out there. Women have always been given a lower position and a lower role in life. Sometimes justice will actually be done in this life, but don't count on it. The important thing is that we can teach our children to submit with the hope that God will make all things right.

Submission is a learned response. It is supposed to be taught at home in the form of obedience. Children must be taught to obey all authority figures. The sooner this lesson is learned the easier it is on everyone: the child; the parent; the teachers; etc..

In the same passage which I alluded to before, we also see that the man is supposed to love his wife as Christ loved the Church and laid His life down for her. It would be so peaceful if the husbands and the wives would just maintain their roles as spelled out to them, in God's book.

Some men have mistakenly taken some of the words of this passage out of context and have built their own doctrine of slave/master relationship.

Not if men would do what God commands. In many marriages the husband has set himself up as "Donny Dictator" and believes that everyone should bow and scrape before him. This could not be any further from the truth. If husbands would only follow the instructions found in God's word, The Bible, women would be overjoyed to be married to such a man.

In all of this, the children are expected to submit to the authority of the parents. If this is not followed, you, as a parent, will have a multitude of problems with the children. Someday, you may even stand at the judgment seat of God and have to give HIM and account for why you messed up this child's life when you neglected to enforce discipline, respect, and submission.

True submission should really be a heart attitude. It should come from an attitude of love for the person you are submitting to. If your children are to submit to your authority, you must be a loving parent. True love sometimes says, NO.

As a twelve ear old, Jesus was teaching in the Temple. The doctors of the law were hanging on his every word. This could have been a very "heady" experience with anyone else but Jesus Christ. When His parents found Him, He went back quietly with them to Nazareth. As best we can understand, He lived with them throughout His childhood as an obedient child. Luke 2:52 states the Jesus, "Increased in wisdom and stature". If He increased in wisdom, I submit that He also must have learned to submit to His earthly parents. Let us remember that His parents certainly were just as human as you and I are; especially in the eyes of Jesus, who is and was God.

Certainly it would take no great effort to show that Christ was a "meek" individual. Many adults do not truly understand what the word, "meek" really means. Meekness is related to humility, but it is not the same. To be meek is to not force your will...not to have to always get your own way all the time. Jesus displayed this in a classic way when He was praying in the Garden, before he was to be betrayed. In His prayer, He said what His desires were, but then He followed it up with the beautiful and meek words, "But not my will, but thine be done".

Meekness is when a person with great power, for the sake of others, chooses not to use His power. He displayed it, again, when He allowed the riff-raff to stand at the foot of the cross and challenge Him, the mighty creator, to come down off from the cross. He could, if He were the meek man that we know He was, we knew He wouldn't. It was not the nails that held Jesus Christ on the cross...**IT WAS HIS VERY REAL AND GREAT LOVE FOR US THAT KEPT HIM ON THAT CROSS!** It was the meekness of Christ that saved us from our own punishment.

It is this kind of attitude of love and meekness that you want to instill in your children. It's a matter of getting them to learn what unselfishness really is. A selfish and willful child will never learn to obey from the heart of love and submit from his heart as long as he is allowed to always get his own way!

Again, however, we can force a child to give in and we can cause a child to not get his own way, but have we succeeded in our lesson? I think not. The initiative for sacrificing one's own way and will, need to come from the heart feelings of love which are a part of that child's make-up.

Perhaps some stimuli for teaching this attitude may be needed. Never reward a specific action. In other words, if your child does something un-selfish...such as giving a piece of pie to a little brother, don't make a great big deal out of it and reward the child for this specific action. You can and should, however, do something nice for the child from time to time with this tag line (or something similar): "Johnny, I just wanted you to know that mommy/daddy is really happy with the unselfishness that you have been showing. We just wanted to do something nice for you to show our appreciation for this good behavior".

We give negative forms of discipline for bad behavior, but I really don't believe that enough of us reward good behavior. Please do not misunderstand me...I am not advocating that you reward your child each-and-every-time they do what they are supposed to do (expected to do), but you should...MUST...reward them from time-to-time for the good things that you want to encourage in their lives.

The submission that your child displays should be motivated by love. It is the same reason that husbands should treat their wives well and the same reason that husbands will bend their will to God's. It is the reason that wives will follow, respect, and obey their husbands. This should be the motivating factor in submission found **IN EVERYONE!**

You are going to have to teach your child to replace selfishness with love. Again, Jesus is your standard and the role model that you need to hold up to your child. You need to point out that love involves sacrifice. Point to the cross and explain what Jesus gave up, in heaven, so that we could be freed from all of our sins. Share with your children other sacrificial deeds of love that are found in the Bible and that you might even be able to point out around you (in the newspaper, among friend; relatives, marriage partner, etc..).

For this to work, however, we need to set the example. We need to show a degree of unselfishness in our own daily lives. Your child will pick up on these self-sacrificing moments. Sometimes we treat our children as though they were too slow to see and understand. Your children will surprise you with what they grasp (things you didn't think they noticed). Don't let these things be bad...let them pick up on your display of submission, affection, respect, and obedience to others.

Self control fosters submission. If we can train our children to practice self control, we will see more and more submission in their lives. Take a look at the adults. When our expectations aren't being met by others we still need to control our attitude and continue to have a meek, gentle, and submissive spirit. The reason that this is not done quite as often as we would like, is that we have never learned to do it as a child. We were allowed to get our way and if we didn't get our way, we were allowed to throw a fit of some kind. Adults may still be throwing their "fits".

When others do bad things to us...especially others that we are supposed to submit to, it leaves a bad taste in our mouths and keeps us from displaying a submissive attitude. We need o understand that their bad behavior does not let us off the hook. Wives, you still need to submit to those "selfish, egotistical, and sometimes just plain stupid" husbands of yours. Children still need to submit to their parents, even when those parents are not behaving in a Christ like way. Husbands, you still need to submit to the needs of your wife...even if she is not treating you right. Church member, you still need to submit to the leadership of the Church, even when you can't agree on the decisions that have been made.

If we could set the example and train our children in this respect, we could probably eliminate so many problems in the home, Church, and society, in general. If we don't get this principle across to our children, we and they are going to produce and receive so very many problems in life.

Part of submission is commitment. The wife commits (totally trusts) everything that she has and everything that she is. The man commits his life to the Lord. The child commits his life into the safekeeping of the parents (for a time). Real submission that is from the heart involves giving everything over, in trust, to the one that you will submit to.

You cannot submit to someone that you do not trust. Certainly you will not submit to someone that you doubt and fear. Submission, then, is an act of trust and to some degree...faith: Faith that this person or being is not going to purposely harm you; Faith that this person really does love you and will do their best for you.

Surely you, as a parent, can convince your children that you have only their best interests in mind. If you can't, you are doing something totally wrong. Perhaps you need to sit down with your children and explain what your overall plans and goals are for you and them. Maybe if they could be reassured that you have only their best interests at heart, they would be more readily willing to submit to your authority.

Bringing it to the spiritual level, isn't that why we would submit to God? We know, beyond a shadow of a doubt, that God only wants the very best for us. Because of this, if He asks us to do anything, we would do it (without understanding why). This is submission. We don't have to know why or how it will work...we simply need to know what to do and we will do it.

Perfect submission comes hard and is seldom seen. I believe that it is seldom seen because it is seldom taught and even more seldom practiced in the home. Children are imitators. They do what they see and hear. If you want to teach your children to be submissive to authority, show them how it's done.

Chapter 12
Potpourri

I have entitled this chapter, "Potpourri", because that is exactly what it is. I had many subjects that I wished to deal with, but when I took a close look at them I realized that none of them warranted a full chapter's examination. They do, however, warrant some attention. I will give mini titles to these various thoughts.

ADMIT YOUR FAULTS

One fatal error that I think many parents attempt to do is to impress their children with the false impression that they (the parents) never make mistakes. You, my friend, are NOT perfect. You and I have made many mistakes. Some of these mistakes were no "big deals", but some of our mistakes would dwarf some of our children's worst errors. Do not try to live a lie! Admit to your children that you have made mistakes.

You might explain that you really intended nothing wrong or bad, but we all make mistakes. Seek your children's forgiveness if the mistake affected them, in any way. Be ready to accept the mistakes that your children make, as well. Explain what you have learned by your mistake and lead your child to a learning experience that they have come to by their mistakes, as well.

Admit your mistake as soon as it happens. Do not wait until you are backed into a corner by your sixteen year old child. Try to be the first to recognize your errors. Only when you do this can you expect your children to quickly and honestly recognize their mistakes, as well. If you try, at all, to hide your mistakes, be sure, "Your sins will find you out".

Be merciful to your children in the mistakes that they make. This needs to start at an early age. Spilling the milk from the table to th floor may be upsetting to you, as well as to your child. **YOU NEED TO BE MERCIFUL TO YOUR CHILD**, even as Christ, Jesus is **ALWAYS** merciful to you. After all, this is not the end of the world. As I have said before, let it be a learning tool. Perhaps the lesson might be that we need to put our glass further away from the edge of the table. Maybe the lesson is that we cannot hold a sandwich in one hand and a full glass of milk in the other (at least not at age two).

Show by your words and by your actions that you really are aware of your faults and that you are going to be working on them. There is a bond between parent and child when they can see something in common...even mistakes.

Your example can inspire the proper treatment of those mistakes and a working towards of the solution. Admitting mistakes, confessing, and seeking forgiveness, or granting forgiveness (as the case may be) also becomes a wonderful example and object lesson for our lives, within the plan of God's mercy.

CAREER CHOICE (THE RIGHT ONES)

One thing that parents must understand and accept is that your child's career choice is ultimately his/hers. It is not your career choice and if you operate as though it were, one of two things is going to happen: Your child will not want to include you in his/her plans...or...you will ramrod your child into a career with which he/she will not be truly happy.

Career decisions should not be a vicarious fulfillment of a parent's lost dreams. You had your chance at a career choice. If you made a mistake, try to change it. If you can't change it, live with it. But, please don't try to live your life's dream through your child.

In making the choice, as to career selection, help your child obtain **ALL** of the facts. Let the child point to the potential career and then help him/her do the proper research. Intelligent decisions are not going to be based on emotions, hype, or pipe dreams. The better the research, the less of a chance that the child will be disappointed in his/her selection.

Early on, in the child's development, try to explain what kind of jobs would **NOT** be good choices for a Christian. Your child should not even be considering a job as a bar tender, a carney, a bookie, etc…These are quite obvious but there are some that are not so immediately obvious. For instance: If you are a Christian and Church attendance is important to you and you are trying to instill that importance in you child, you and the child may want to use this as a standard criteria in considering a career. Does this career take a person away from the Church for extended periods of time: Hopefully your child will make a decision to **NOT** pursue that career if it does take him away from the things of the Church.

Expose your child to a wide variety of career choices. This variety may expose your child to a career that he would never have thought of, but one in which he is really interested (once the student knows about it).

In the end, lend as much support as possible to your child's choice. You may not especially like your child's choice, but as long as it is not unethical, immoral, illegal, or wicked in any other way…you need to support him/her in that decision. Remember parents, it's **NOT ABOUT YOU.**

CHOOSE YOUR BATTLES

There are so many things that you, as a parent, need to deal with. Sometimes, however, we think that we have to address **EVERY** possible problem. This is not to say that we don't need to deal with problems, but what I am saying is this: "Choose your battles". Everything doesn't need to be dealt with. Some things are relatively unimportant and quite insignificant. Make sure that this is where you want to "draw the line" in the sand.

If you must step in and do battle, **KNOW WHAT YOU ARE TALKING ABOUT!!** All too often I have started to deal with what I perceived was a problem, only to find out that I was completely wrong about my facts about the issue. Egg on the face sure does look funny and crow tastes awful.

Perhaps a few simple self-examination questions would relieve us of a lot of embarrassment: 1.) Is anyone being placed in any danger (now or possibly as a result of some action on the part of the child)? 2.) Is this a violation of the rules that have been spelled out?

(You may have to go over the rule again with the student). 3.) Am I in control of my emotions in dealing with this? 4.) Have I overlooked this same thing in the past?

There may be some other questions that you can think of to ask yourself. The point is this: Don't jump in to fast...don't "shoot from the hip". Remain calm and thoughtful when you are dealing with children. The older that they become, the more important this is (and the harder it is to practice).

There are some subjects that my wife and I chose not to confront or "deal with": Their music (as long as they have religious lyrics and are not played in our presence). Music is totally subjective. A lot depends on the baggage that a person brings to the table. If one has grown up in the sixties, one finds certain instruments, sounds, and beats still offensive. We are offended by what we associate those things with. Our children never encountered any of this. To them it is simply a good religious song. You, as a parent can begin a long (and an ultimately lost) war over "Christian" music.

Choose your battles. If you are going to fight "Christian rock", **YOU WILL LOSE!** Save your energy for the "Big Ones".

What we were concerned with was not so much the music, but the lifestyle of the singers and the musicians. We did discuss the subject of: Becoming slaves to trends and styles (in music, in clothing, in anything). We were concerned with and pointed out to our teens, the message that these musicians were sending, **LOUD AND CLEAR**. The overall question that we tried to get across was: "What is this music doing for you spiritual growth"?

Another thing that we did not fuss about is clothing styles. It may not be something that we would want to wear, but as long as it was modest, clean, and did not give the wrong impression to the opposite sex, it passed.

THE KEYS TO THE CAR

Now we come to what can be a parental thorn in the side. Teen agers want to drive. They need to understand; from the very beginning that driving is a double privilege. The state says that driving is a privilege which they will grant to responsible citizens as long as the citizen will remain responsible.

Mom and Dad say that driving is a privilege which their children may exercise as long as mom and dad allow it! The state can and will take away **ANYONE'S** driving privilege for offenses against the law. Mom and Dad reserve the right to take away a child's privilege for **ANY REASON, WHATSOEVER!!**

Taking away a child's driving privilege may not be especially connected to bad driving practices. This privilege may be taken away as a punishment connected to something totally unrelated to driving. We must remember, however, that this is a **MAJOR** form of punishment and should be used with a good deal of thought and care. It really should be regarded as a "last resort".

Driving privileges may also be taken away, even if the state doesn't do it, for violations that are done with the car. For instance: Your child is making donuts in the grocery store's parking lot after the store is closed. This lot may have many light poles in it and your child is subjecting **YOUR** car to the possibility of a major accident. If you have already told your child to **NOT** do this...even though the law didn't catch him but you did. You need to make up your mind as to the punishment for this child's disobedience.

Some rules that need to be laid down (these rules are up to the parent's discretion) are as follows: 1.) Never is there to be a display of anger while driving your car (no "peeling out" in anger; no speeding around corners in anger; not any other type of reckless and/or careless driving as a result of anger). 2.) No speeding (even if **NOT** angry). 3.) No fooling around behind the wheel. Your child needs to get the idea that driving is **ALWAYS A VERY SERIOUS AFFAIR!**

These rules and any other rules you make, apply to your child whether driving your car of his own car. If your child is living under your roof, they are to abide by your rules. If they are under age, the law says that they must abide by your rules. If they are eighteen years old (or older) they must abide by your rules, or move out.

Define in clear terms, what punishment will be meted out for different infractions. You must be ready to take away the keys and/or the license, if necessary. Know this; it may not just be your child that is involved. His/her dangerous driving habits endanger everyone else on the highway. If you are not ready to live with yourself if you child should kill or injure someone else because of their foolish actions, then **ENFORCE THE RULES!**

Encourage financial responsibility. It is all right to help your child financially but there is no such thing as a "free ride" in life, doesn't try to invent the free ride here. Your child needs to pay for the gasoline, the insurance or the car. (You might choose to burden them with one of these three things, or all three...**IT IS YOUR JUDGEMENT!**). Make sure that your child knows that they will be held financially accountable.

Very important: **WITHOUT FAIL, YOU PARENTS MUST KNOW AND LIMIT ALL PERMISSIBLE PASSENGERS...AT ALL TIMES!** Make sure that **YOU** lay the law down to those passengers and let them know the consequences to their friend (you child) if they should violate your rules. Young people (and many adults do not realize the danger in just the sheer fact that they are moving at high speeds with a two to three thousand pound piece of steel. Just a little "cutting up" in that car by those passengers or that driver can result in **DEATH!**

COMMUNICATION—A TWO WAY STREET

We, as parents, need to all go to "listening school". So much of the time we are to busy talking and we just do not listen. Listening is not just done with the ears. It is done with the understanding... with the heart. The old saying goes this way, "God gave us two ears and only one mouth"...I wonder why? James 1:19 says it this way "Let every man (and woman) be **SWIFT TO HEAR**, slow to speak, and slow to wrath".

A good way to make sure that you are really listening with understanding is to echo what you have heard, "Let me get this straight, you are saying..."? You will find that quite often you really did not hear what was actually said. We often hear what we **THINK** someone is saying. Perhaps we are too busy forming an answer and we just don't listen all the way.

Keep the lines of communications open. If you start at an early age, your child will continue to carry on conversations with you through their teen years. The best way to foster this kind of communications is to talk about things of interest to your children while you are conducting "devotions", and to listen when they want to talk, even if you are busy (unless they are interrupting another conversation).

Let the child understand that his/her thoughts are important and have some validity. Answer their questions. This can be a real challenge when they are very young. Little children can ask ten thousand questions per day. If you are very wise, you will answer all ten thousand questions that are asked. If you answer these questions, the child will learn **EVEN IN THEIR TEEN YEARS** that they can ask questions of Mom and Dad. You will become their confidant. Part of the questions are just curiosity, but part of this is a test to see if you consider them important. Don't blow your chances for a good relationship with your child by short changing them in this area. The same goes for teens when they are using you as a "sounding board" but are not really looking for solutions.

If you need to criticize your child, do it constructively. Do not just tell the child what they have done wrong. Give your child some working suggestions as to how they may make decisions and corrections. Treat your child with dignity. Even if he/she has done something wrong does not make them the "lowest sink hole in the earth".

As much as possible, speak in soft tones. The book of Psalms tells us that a "soft answer turns away wrath". It turns away bitterness and resentment as well. Speak to your child in the same manner that you would like to be spoken to. You, as a parent, can get a lot more accomplished with soft and gentle words than you will ever accomplish by shouting and nagging.

BED WETTING

I almost had enough material to write a full chapter on this subject, but I decided to not go into as much depth as I originally planned. This is a subject that is near and dear to parents with toddlers (and sometimes all the way up into their teen years...talk about a self esteem destroyer!).

Let me start by giving some good and real reasons that your child wets the bed. Some of you have been told (or believe) that this is the reason(s) that they wet the bed: 1.) Your child does not wet the bed because he is lazy. 2.) He is not stubborn and rebellious. They would like to stop wetting their beds probably more than you do. 3.) They do not like to see you get excited and scream at them. Believe it or not...they really wish that you would STOP SCREAMING AT THEM! 4.) They really don't wet the bed so that you will have to do more washing. More than likely they don't even think of this angle unless you bring it up. 5.) They do not wet the bed as a test to see how much fluid a standard mattress can hold. It can hold plenty and I don't think that they can produce enough to completely water log their mattress. 6.) They definitely do not wet the bed because they like the smell of urine. **THEY ABSOLUTELY ABHOR THE SMELL OF URINE!** Not only is this a disgusting smell, but it is also the smell of failure.

Your children wet the bed for the following reason(s): 1.) The bladder is not yet fully developed and able to hold a large capacity. Perhaps you can remember this fact when you allow him to drink a forty-four ounce drink. 2.) Your child wets the bed because of **YOUR GENES AND CHROMOSOMES!!** If it's anyone's fault, **IT'S MOST PROBABLY YOURS.** This child has inherited, from you, something called "deep sleep". Chances are that you also did wet the bed when you were a child because you also inherited this "deep sleep" pattern from your parents. The "deep sleep" pattern cannot be corrected without the intervention of a doctor. While I am on the subject of doctors…**I AM NOT ONE AND DO NOT WISH THAT YOU WOULD TAKE WHAT I WRITE AS BONA FIDE MEDICAL ADVICE!**

There is an excellent possibility that your child will outgrow this problem (just as you have). It does take time, however, and it takes patience on your part. If you really cannot deal with all of this, contact someone who can help you (medically). **PLEASE, UNDER NO CIRCUMSTANCES TAKE IT OUT ON YOUR CHILD!!!**

You may find that finances would dictate that an expert might even be cheaper than the replacement of the mattress and sheets, over and over. If you opt to not seek out an expert, get a **GOOD** and thick plastic cover. **DO NOT SCRIMP IN THIS.** The cover is still cheaper than the mattress or the doctor. You might do best by picking up a good cover at some "garage sale". Of course you can find replacement sheets at these "garage sales" as well.

Something that helped with our children is that we noticed if we awakened the child at about five or six a.m. and had them go to the bathroom, they would not wet the bed. I know that this takes some special effort, but you must decide: 1.) Setting the alarm clock and putting the child on the "potty". Or 2.) Facilitating the ruining the child's self-esteem, replacing mattress and sheets.

NEVER DISCUSS THIS PROBLEM IN FRONT OF THE CHILD'S SIBLINGS OR ANYONE ELSE, FOR THAT MATTER!!!!

All of this is **EXTREMELY** personal and really, to the **MAX**, embarrassing. Respect your loved one's self respect and esteem and keep it private and personal.

Remember this; you were probably a bed wetter also. You know the hurt that you felt, as a child. Your parents may not have dealt with this problem correctly. It was because they really didn't know. This is not your excuse, now. If you were not a bed wetter, try to understand and empathize with the child that you profess to love. Have mercy on your child, please.

GOD FILLS IN ALL OF THE BLANKS

I do believe that this is the most important part of this book. That is why have saved it for the end. We are not perfect beings. No matter how conscientious we may be, we will make mistakes. Some of our mistakes can even be catastrophic. We may not even be able to forgive ourselves for some of our mistakes. Let me tell you, if you are a Christian, **FORGIVE YOURSELF...GOD DID, DOES, AND WILL CONTINUE TO FORGIVE YOU.**

We are told in the Sacred Scriptures to: "Train up a child in the way he should go and when he is old, he will not depart from it". If you could do this perfectly from the perspective of a perfect being all would be well. The problem arises, however, when our children dwell on our imperfections and mistakes. Sometimes they use these mistakes for justification in doing wrong.

Be encouraged in this thought: God will help you by adjusting the thinking of the child when and if that child becomes obedient to the Lord. If you can do a good job in instilling good, spiritual values in your children, many of your mistakes will be absorbed by that very child...later in life.

Also, know that God has already helped you by giving you children with which He knows you can work. If you could not possibly handle a "strong-willed-child", He would not have blessed you with one. Nothing happens by accident when we deal with God. God is at the helm and is steering your life (to some extent and with your cooperation). If you can look at child rearing in this light, you **CAN** be encouraged.

God has built into every family a forgiveness factor. Children can forgive a lot of mistakes. God will forgive a lot of mistakes. Do the best that you can, lean on God for direction, and you will do fine. Remember, this book was not written by one whom did everything right. It is written by one who made a lot of mistakes and has learned by them.

Chapter 13
Some General Thought in Raising Children in Christ

Hey, nobody said that it would be easy. There are many reasons for having children. Some of the reasons make sense; some will even bring tears to our eyes. Some of the reasons are pathetic, and sometimes you might wish that there was such a thing as a "good sense cop" in instances where people seem to have lost their brains.

Some of the worst reasons are selfish reasons. You know the stories. Mother gets pregnant to increase the welfare check (thankfully this isn't so easy to do anymore). One or both parties in a marriage have children to try and "cement" their failing marriage. A variation on this theme: She gets pregnant because she thinks that a baby will keep him from leaving (often used in "shack jobs"). Finally (not because we have run out of stupid reasons to have children, but for the sake of time and paper), she thinks that a baby would fulfill her emotional needs.

Raising children is an unselfish task. It takes a whole of giving, and for a while, not much "getting". When we attempt to raise children we must understand that the real beginning starts approximately nine months before. Moms need to go through some of the most excruciating pain known to humans. Then Moms (and sometimes, Dads) get up at all hours of the night and early morning to feed and change our "bundle of joy". We can also include emergency runs to the hospital or doctor because our little one has fallen badly, or has a temp of 105. All through childhood and teen years, parents must be ready to sacrifice for approximately eighteen years (or until all of the children have left the nest).

Raising children properly may interfere with your job, to some extent. This does not usually affect the wife and mother so much as it affects the husband and the DAD. Sometimes we see Mom taking on a job, outside the home, this often is the case when she feels that she wants or feels that she needs another job or even a career.

So many men identify their worth with what they "produce" for the family. They feel that their main function in life is to put food on the table; provide transportation; keep the family in shoes and clothing; and perhaps provide the financial where-with-all for the annual vacation.

Indeed, and to some extent, these things are perceived as "necessary"...certainly are wanted. Never should ANY of these things be at the expense of the family. We will deal with "Time Management" later on in this book.

We now come to the twenty-first century predicament: A two bread winner family. 1.) The man has such a low skill level that he has to work long hours for less money as the college graduate. Things may be so bad that he may even need to work two jobs. 2.) One partner may inherit the other partner's debts that were incurred before they were married. 3.) Both parties may be attempting to become "debt free". 4.) The "wanter button" is stuck and all this couple can do is "want" and "spend".

Humans can and do attempt to justify what is flat out wrong! Just remember, God did not intend a family where EVERYONE has to work. The main reason everyone has to work is everyone likes to buy. If this type of setup is followed for very long, the children will suffer in many ways, remember, earlier on, that I said that when we have children we will be called upon to sacrifice...cutting spending, weaning off second jobs, bringing Mama home, these are all part of the suffering that I was referring to.

It is quite popular in this day and age to want to pay off all debt and become "debt free". This is noble and in keeping with the scriptures (owe no man anything except love). But so are some strong admonishments for the proper raising of children. Which one do we ignore? Neither. The thing is, though, that we need to compromise a little on the debt paying and for a short time, probably compromise a little for a short time on the proper care of our children.

You say, "I'll never compromise"! If that is your stand, then you tell me how you are going to fix the mess that you got yourself in. The compromise route **CAN ONLY BE FOR A SHORT TIME!** We need to work our very best to bring the proper solution to our dilemma. Understand this; God's Word **DOES** say that the woman's role is in the home. It is mankind's overspending that has made it necessary for both to feel that they **MUST WORK** outside the home.

Also understand that you will probably put some "dents" in your credit rating. You may even ruin you credit. I would rather see you ruin your credit rating than for you to ruin your family.

Will you have a "House Beautiful" or a "House Lived In"? The number one priority in your home needs to be: comfort; safety; and security. To some degree a Mom will try to have the children play the more destructive games outdoors. This cannot always be done. Everyone has cold days; snowy days; rainy days; etc..

We just need to "child proof" the house or make very clear rules of things not to do or touch in the house. A home should be warm and "snuggly" as possible. Warm in the winter and cool in the summer. Long ago we should have come to an understanding that one of the main functions of the house is to raise our children. Is it more important to have toy free rooms or to have happy and well developed children? Can you really believe for a moment that you may be subject to be cast into hell because you kept a slightly cluttered warm and snuggly home?

You may live in a house, but you provide a home. A home is where one can relax and not feel threatened. A home is where you can make a mess and it doesn't always need to be cleaned up right away (unless something of importance is threatened by it). A home is where you can not only be warmed by a fire, but also by the love and the care of two parents and children. Home is where you take your bath and where you get bedside stories read to you. Home is where you can pray with Mom and Dad. There is something very special about a home for a child. No child should have to live in mortal danger of spills; scuff marks; breakage; etc...This is not to say that rules cannot be made and discipline enforced when it comes to the upkeep of the house. The problem, as I see it, is that there are those who are more embarrassed by a lived in house than by the fact that their children cannot "live" in their own home.

For you to expect that your house will always remain a "Good Housekeeping" showcase is totally unreal and impractical. By sacrificing neatness, you will receive a far greater reward when you see your children laughing; running; jumping; shouting (in fun); and just generally well adjusted.

Just realize this: There are some parents in this world who would gladly welcome the chance for their children to run and bump into things. Perhaps their children don't have the use of their legs. Other parents would love to hear their children laugh and shout. Their children may not be capable of such natural exercises. Then there is the couple who would give **ANYTHING** to be able to even have children, at all. Give God thanks each day for your children, and be ready and totally willing to sacrifice your comfort and your idea of orderliness so that they might grow up well adjusted and healthy. That they would have a lifetime of happy memories of Mom and Dad.

Try to engender an interest in some of the same things that you do. You want to simply be creating the same interests in you children and in the process, you may be creating "partners" in that same interest. What a great reward you will reap when those little "ankle biters" become teen agers and can join you as equals in the same fun things that you like.

Relaxation sports may also have to be placed on the sacrificial altar. If you cannot include your children in those sports, you may have to curtail a regular enjoyment of them. As has been mentioned, you could teach your little one how to play golf or tennis. The problem arises when you may have two or three little ones and they do not at all like you relaxation sport. Then again, if you have taught them to join you ever since they could first walk, they may not even know that they don't enjoy it.

It is possible that you could take the one(s) that do like it out one day and the one(s) that don't to some other relaxation sport another day. Remember...**THE WORD IS SACRIFICE!** Time is the thing that is going to be burnt up on this altar.

The children have to be the most important thing in this equation. What if none of the children like your favorite relaxation sport?

This is not to say that you will **NEVER AGAIN ALLOWED TO BOWL OR PLAY TENNIS OR PLAY GOLF.** You don't **ABSOLUTELY NEED TO PLAY THESE SPORTS OR YOU WILL DIE!** When the kids leave the nest you can take them up again... **WITH A VENGEANCE!** The real point is this: Your children need their Mommy and their Daddy.

Made in the USA
Columbia, SC
20 August 2021